2261

2261

S0-CAF-237

Christmas is Coming!

VOL. 4

Compiled and Edited
by Shannon L. Sexton

Oxmoor House®

page 80

©1994 by Oxmoor House, Inc.
Book Division of Southern Progress Corporation
P.O. Box 2463, Birmingham, Alabama 35201

Published by Oxmoor House, Inc., and Leisure Arts, Inc.

All rights reserved. No part of this book may be
reproduced in any form or by any means without the prior
written permission of the publisher, excepting brief
quotations in connection with reviews written specifically
for inclusion in magazines or newspapers, or single copies
for strictly personal use.

Library of Congress Catalog Card Number: 94-65475
Softcover ISBN: 0-8487-1414-8
Softcover ISSN: 1074-8954
Manufactured in the United States of America
First Printing

Editor-in-Chief: Nancy J. Fitzpatrick
Senior Crafts Editor: Susan Ramey Wright
Senior Editor, Editorial Services: Olivia Kindig Wells
Art Director: James Boone

Christmas is Coming! Vol. 4

Editor: Shannon L. Sexton
Editorial Assistant: Rhonda Richards Wamble
Illustrator and Designer: Barbara Ball
Copy Editor: L. Amanda Owens
Copy Assistant: Leslee Rester Johnson
Senior Photographer: John O'Hagan
Photostylist: Connie Formby
Associate Production Manager: Theresa L. Beste
Production Assistant: Marianne Jordan

Contents

Adventures at Camp Kringle Jingle

page 108

Children's Workshop: Happy Holiday Crafts

Trimmings to Fix

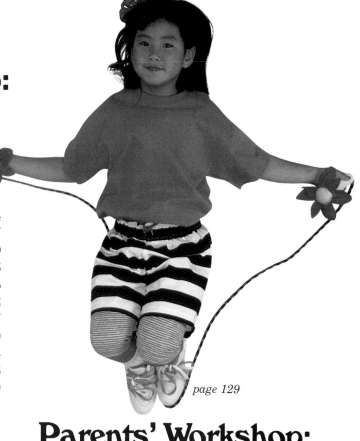

Presents to Make

Parents' Workshop: Great Gifts for Children

Grin and Wear It

Just for Fun

Designers & Contributors

Dear Kids,

Calling all campers! Have you ever attended a summer camp or a day camp? If so, chances are you remember games, crafts, and delicious treats! And that's just what you'll find at my special Christmas camp—Camp Kringle Jingle. Turn the page to discover the excitement waiting for you and to meet me, your camp counselor Kringle Jingle. I'll lead you into the action with games such as **Santa-Sack Relay**, **Kringle Hop**, and **Go Fish!** We'll make nifty projects like a **Twinkle Tote** backpack and **Twig Tree** decorations. You're sure to work up an appetite after all of this fun, so I created **Kringle Eats 'n' Treats** full of mouth-watering morsels like **Chocolate-Covered Snowballs**.

"Trimmings to Fix" shows you how to really get ready for Santa. **Lighten Up** with a strand of giant colored lights or **Make an Impression** by designing your own Christmas card. Treat your dog and cat to **Pet Stockings** shaped like a bone and a mouse. Then turn to "Presents to Make" for a pet-pleasing stocking stuffer, **Crunchy Pet Cookies**. And if you need gift ideas, "Presents to Make" is the place to look. Decorate a planter for Mom using neat paper napkins. Whip up a message center for Dad with foam shapes and clothespins. Or for friends, make hand-painted, funky reindeer pins.

Be sure to check with a grown-up before you begin. Then get busy because **Christmas is Coming!**

Your Camp Counselor,
Kringle Jingle

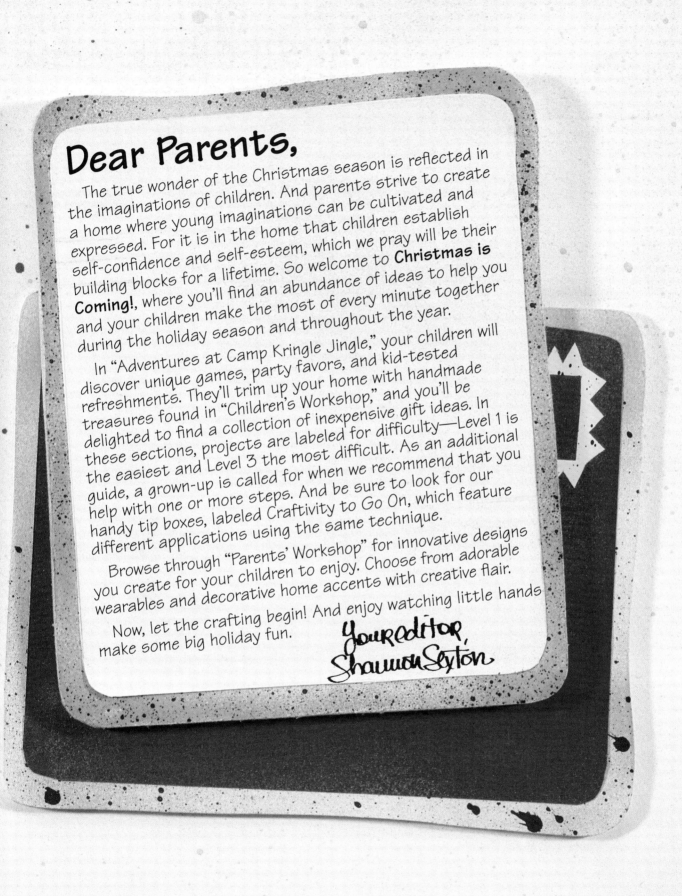

Dear Parents,

The true wonder of the Christmas season is reflected in the imaginations of children. And parents strive to create a home where young imaginations can be cultivated and expressed. For it is in the home that children establish self-confidence and self-esteem, which we pray will be their building blocks for a lifetime. So welcome to **Christmas is Coming!**, where you'll find an abundance of ideas to help you and your children make the most of every minute together during the holiday season and throughout the year.

In "Adventures at Camp Kringle Jingle," your children will discover unique games, party favors, and kid-tested refreshments. They'll trim up your home with handmade treasures found in "Children's Workshop," and you'll be delighted to find a collection of inexpensive gift ideas. In these sections, projects are labeled for difficulty—Level 1 is the easiest and Level 3 the most difficult. As an additional guide, a grown-up is called for when we recommend that you help with one or more steps. And be sure to look for our handy tip boxes, labeled Craftivity to Go On, which feature different applications using the same technique.

Browse through "Parents' Workshop" for innovative designs you create for your children to enjoy. Choose from adorable wearables and decorative home accents with creative flair.

Now, let the crafting begin! And enjoy watching little hands make some big holiday fun.

Your editor,
Shannon Sexton

Adventures at Camp Kringle Jingle

The Camp Kringle Jingle

Over the river and through the woods
To Camp Kringle Jingle we go . . . .
There I'll show you the way to make merry each day
While you wait for Santa's sleigh, hey!

Over the river and through the woods
To Camp Kringle Jingle we go . . . .
There's camp gear for you and fun games, too
So gather some pals to play, hey!

Over the river and through the woods
To Camp Kringle Jingle we go . . . .
We'll make kringle eats and crafty treats
To share with friends today, hey!

Kringle Jingle Sweatshirt

Try on this animated character for size! This sweatshirt, featuring our Christmas camp counselor, Kringle Jingle, is made using a transfer pencil and fabric crayons.

You will need:
A grown-up
Transfer pencil
2 sheets of white paper
Purchased white sweatshirt
Iron
Fabric crayons

1. Using the transfer pencil, trace the pattern onto 1 sheet of paper.

2. Place the sweatshirt on a flat surface. Center the pattern facedown on the sweatshirt. **Ask the grown-up** to iron the pattern onto the sweatshirt, following the manufacturer's instructions. Remove the paper.

3. Using the fabric crayons, color Kringle Jingle as indicated.

4. Ask the grown-up to cover the colored design with the clean sheet of paper and, following the manufacturer's instructions, iron over the design to set the dyes.

Craftivity to Go On
Reduce or enlarge the Kringle Jingle pattern and transfer it onto boxer shorts, pillowcases, T-shirts, aprons, or tote bags.

9

Twinkle Tote

The nighttime skies over Camp Kringle Jingle inspired campers to decorate their backpacks. Add some star quality to yours, too, and you'll be ready to hike the roughest terrain or to carry a heavy load of books to school.

Level 1

You will need:
Tracing paper
Pencil
Scissors
¼ yard each of felt: gold, yellow
Fabric glue
Purchased canvas backpack

1. Trace and cut out the patterns.

2. For each star, trace 2 star patterns of varying sizes onto different colors of felt. Cut them out. Repeat to make as many stars as desired.

3. To finish each star, center and glue a small star on top of a large star.

4. Arrange the stars on the backpack as desired and glue them in place. Do not cover any zippers or snaps. Let the glue dry.

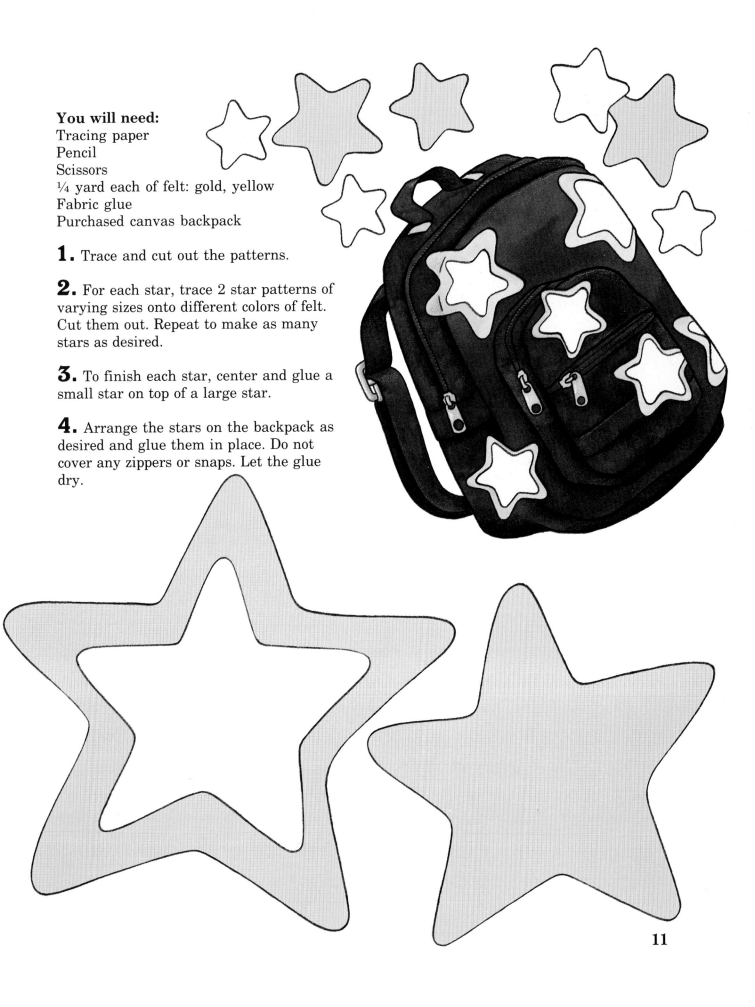

Autograph Pillowcase

My
Camp
Friends

Jazz up a pillowcase with sponge-painted squares and trees. Then have your friends autograph it for a fun souvenir of your next camping trip or slumber party.

You will need:
Tracing paper
Black felt marker
Scissors
Ruler
5″ x 5″ x 1¾″ pop-up sponge
Water-soluble marker
Standard pillowcase
Cardboard covered with waxed paper to fit pillowcase
Fabric paint: yellow, red, green
3 paper plates
Green fabric marker

1. Using the felt marker, trace the pattern block onto the tracing paper. Cut it out along the broken line. Then trace and cut out 1 square and 1 tree pattern. Set them aside.

2. Slide the cardboard between the 2 layers of the pillowcase. Slide the pattern block under the top layer of the pillowcase and into the lower left corner, 2″ from the side edge and 1½″ from the bottom edge. Using the water-soluble marker, trace the pattern block onto the pillowcase. Move

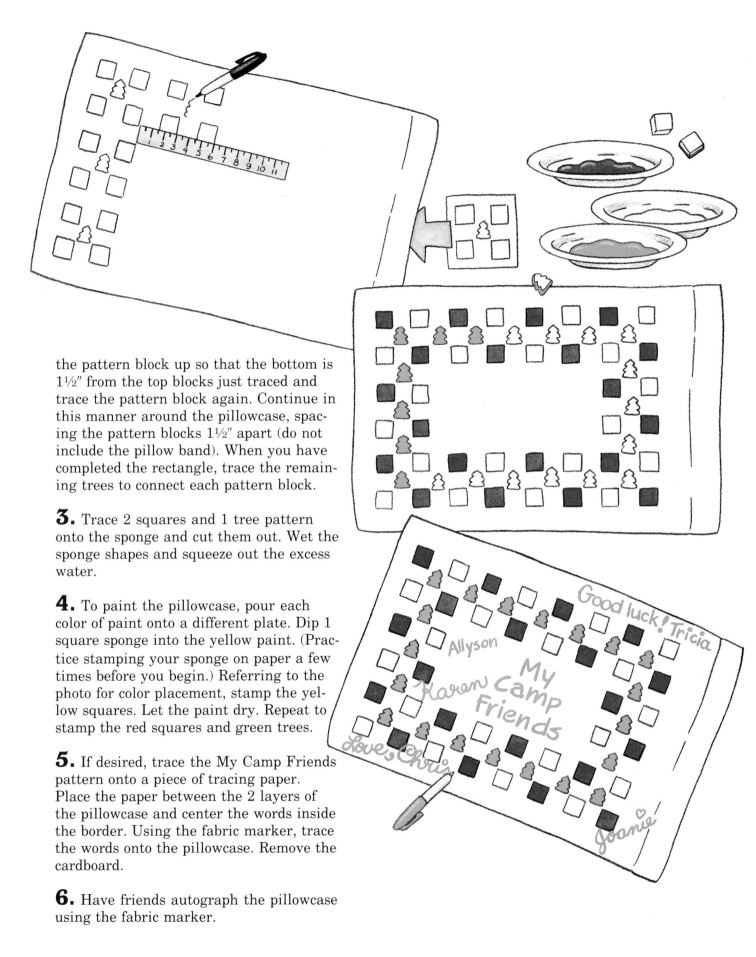

the pattern block up so that the bottom is 1½″ from the top blocks just traced and trace the pattern block again. Continue in this manner around the pillowcase, spacing the pattern blocks 1½″ apart (do not include the pillow band). When you have completed the rectangle, trace the remaining trees to connect each pattern block.

3. Trace 2 squares and 1 tree pattern onto the sponge and cut them out. Wet the sponge shapes and squeeze out the excess water.

4. To paint the pillowcase, pour each color of paint onto a different plate. Dip 1 square sponge into the yellow paint. (Practice stamping your sponge on paper a few times before you begin.) Referring to the photo for color placement, stamp the yellow squares. Let the paint dry. Repeat to stamp the red squares and green trees.

5. If desired, trace the My Camp Friends pattern onto a piece of tracing paper. Place the paper between the 2 layers of the pillowcase and center the words inside the border. Using the fabric marker, trace the words onto the pillowcase. Remove the cardboard.

6. Have friends autograph the pillowcase using the fabric marker.

13

My Camp Friends

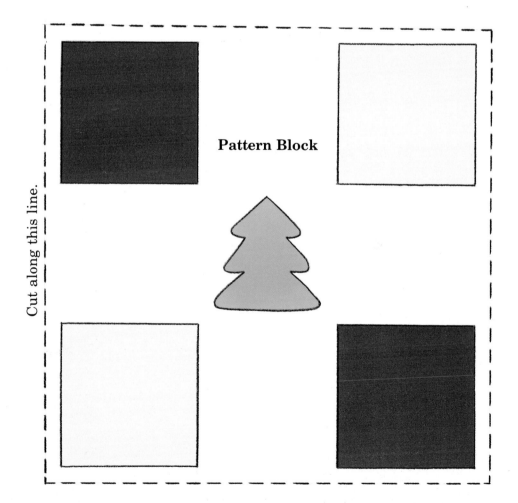

Cut along this line.

Pattern Block

Go Fish!

The excellent fishing at Camp Kringle Jingle lures many visitors, but don't expect a seafood supper. These fishermen hang their prize catches on the Christmas tree! Make a dozen of these fanciful fish and gather your buddies for a unique game of Go Fish.

You will need (for 12 fish):
Tracing paper
Pencil
Scissors
Fun Foam in assorted colors
Paint pens in assorted colors
12 plastic ball ornaments in assorted
  colors
Founder's Adhesive glue
24 (15-mm) wiggle eyes

1. Trace and cut out the patterns. Trace the patterns onto the foam as indicated and cut them out.

2. For each fish, use the paint pens to draw stripes on 1 side of the side fins and on both sides of the top fins and the tails as indicated. Set them aside.

3. Position the ornament so that the hanger attachment is to 1 side. Using the paint pen, start at the center top and draw 3 V shapes on each side. Color in the design with the paint pen. Let the paint dry.

4. Glue 1 wiggle eye on each side of the ornament near the hanger attachment (see photo).

5. Glue 2 side fins, 1 top fin, and 1 tail onto the ornament as shown. Let the glue dry. Repeat for the remaining fish.

You will need (for 2 fishing poles):
A grown-up
Waxed paper
2 (36″ x ⅜″) wooden dowels
Yellow spray paint
3¾ yards (¼″-wide) red grosgrain ribbon
  for fishing line
Scissors
Pencil
Ruler
Founder's Adhesive glue
2 (18″ x 7″) blue Fun Foam sheets
4 rubber bands
2 large ornament hangers
2 small split shot fishing weights
Large plastic bucket for fish game
Blue or green plastic wrap for water

1. Cover your work surface with waxed paper.

2. Ask the grown-up to help you spray-paint the dowels. Let the paint dry. Measure and mark the dowel at 9″ intervals.

3. Cut the ribbon in half. For each pole: To make the fishing line, glue 1 end of 1 ribbon strip to 1 end of the dowel. Loop the ribbon and glue it at the marked points as shown. Let the glue dry.

4. For the handle, cover 1 side of 1 foam sheet with glue. Align 1 short edge of the foam with 1 end of the dowel as shown. Tightly roll the foam around the dowel. Wrap 2 rubber bands around the foam to hold it in place. Let the glue dry and then remove the rubber bands.

5. To make the hook, tie 1 ornament hanger to the end of the ribbon tail. Attach a weight to the ribbon 3″ up from the hook. Repeat for the remaining pole.

6. Fill the bucket with the plastic wrap.

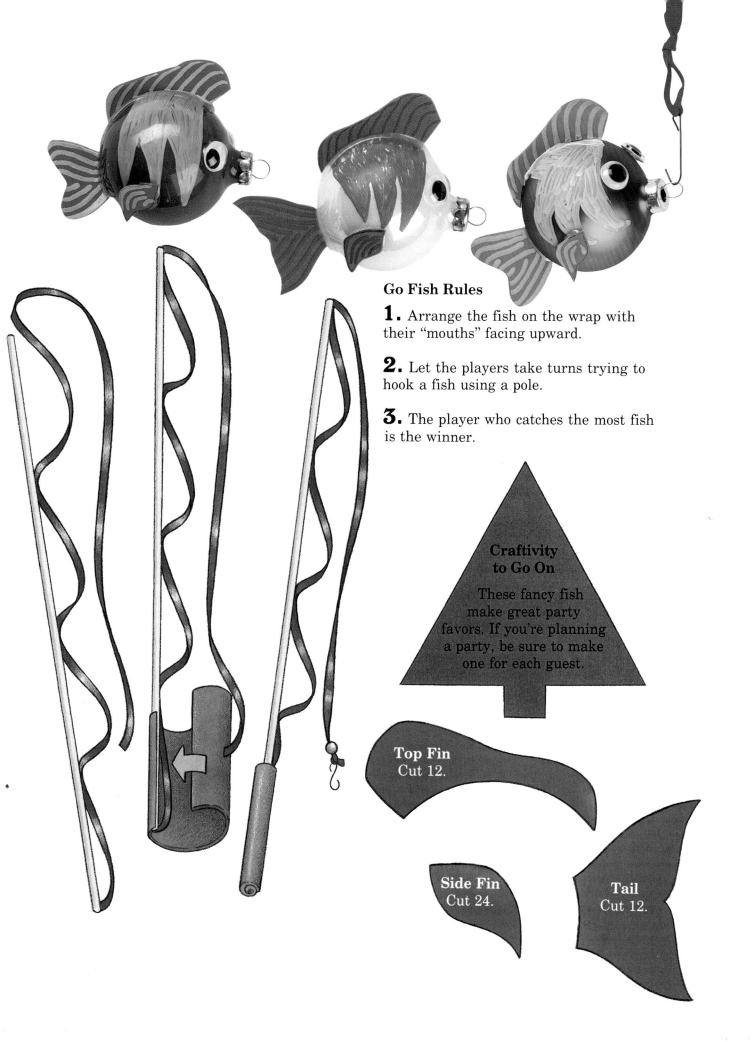

Go Fish Rules

1. Arrange the fish on the wrap with their "mouths" facing upward.

2. Let the players take turns trying to hook a fish using a pole.

3. The player who catches the most fish is the winner.

Craftivity to Go On

These fancy fish make great party favors. If you're planning a party, be sure to make one for each guest.

Top Fin
Cut 12.

Side Fin
Cut 24.

Tail
Cut 12.

Santa-Sack Relay

At the Camp Kringle Jingle Raceway, kids suit up in Santa Sacks. You can race, too, by simply piecing together strips of fabric like a puzzle and gluing them to a laundry bag. Then follow the rules to jump start the fun for an exciting game you and your friends can play anytime.

19

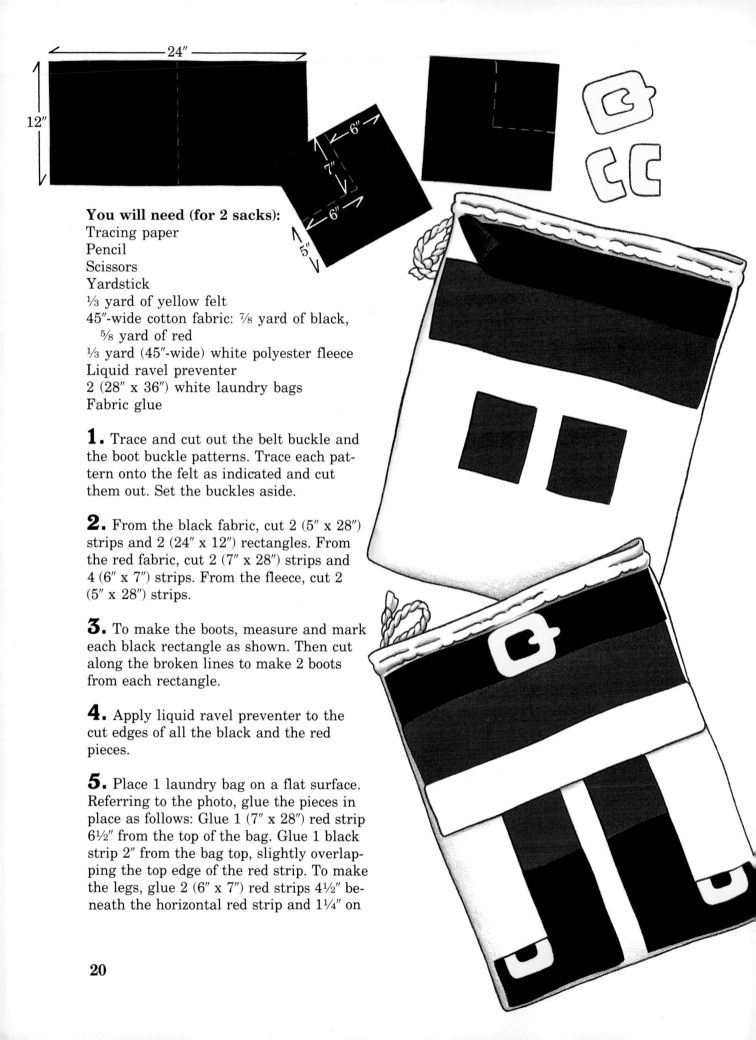

You will need (for 2 sacks):
Tracing paper
Pencil
Scissors
Yardstick
⅓ yard of yellow felt
45″-wide cotton fabric: ⅞ yard of black,
  ⅝ yard of red
⅓ yard (45″-wide) white polyester fleece
Liquid ravel preventer
2 (28″ x 36″) white laundry bags
Fabric glue

1. Trace and cut out the belt buckle and the boot buckle patterns. Trace each pattern onto the felt as indicated and cut them out. Set the buckles aside.

2. From the black fabric, cut 2 (5″ x 28″) strips and 2 (24″ x 12″) rectangles. From the red fabric, cut 2 (7″ x 28″) strips and 4 (6″ x 7″) strips. From the fleece, cut 2 (5″ x 28″) strips.

3. To make the boots, measure and mark each black rectangle as shown. Then cut along the broken lines to make 2 boots from each rectangle.

4. Apply liquid ravel preventer to the cut edges of all the black and the red pieces.

5. Place 1 laundry bag on a flat surface. Referring to the photo, glue the pieces in place as follows: Glue 1 (7″ x 28″) red strip 6½″ from the top of the bag. Glue 1 black strip 2″ from the bag top, slightly overlapping the top edge of the red strip. To make the legs, glue 2 (6″ x 7″) red strips 4½″ beneath the horizontal red strip and 1¼″ on each side of the bag center. Then glue 1 fleece strip beneath the horizontal red strip, slightly overlapping the bottom edge of the red strip and the tops of the red leg pieces. Glue the boots beneath the legs, slightly overlapping the bottom of the red leg pieces.

Center and glue 1 belt buckle on the black strip. Glue 1 buckle on each boot as indicated. Repeat for the remaining laundry bag.

Santa-Sack Relay Rules

1. Divide into 2 teams, with an equal number of people on each team.

2. Designate a starting line and a turning line. Have a member of each team put on a sack, hop from the starting line to the turning line and back again, and then give the sack to the next person to race.

3. The first team to have all members complete the race wins.

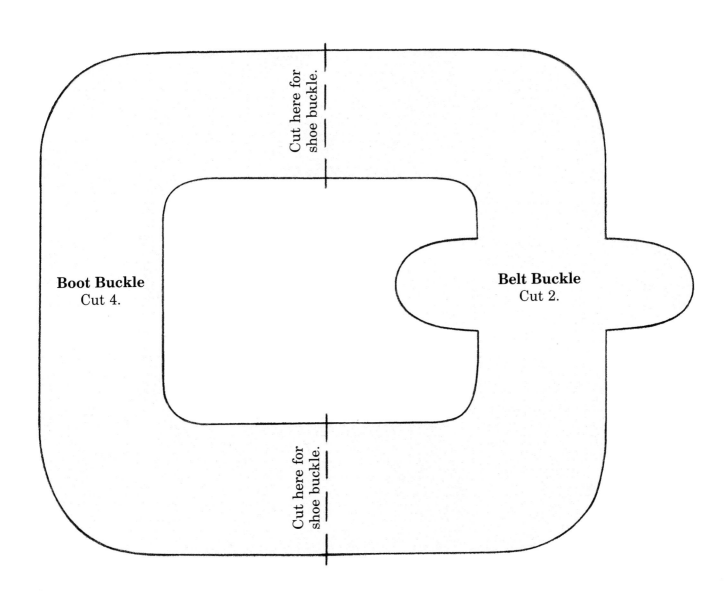

Boot Buckle
Cut 4.

Cut here for shoe buckle.

Cut here for shoe buckle.

Belt Buckle
Cut 2.

Kringle Hop

Making your own hopscotch mat is as easy as 1-2-3! Use your geometric skills to create this colorful mat with triangles, rectangles, and circles. Then do the Kringle Hop!

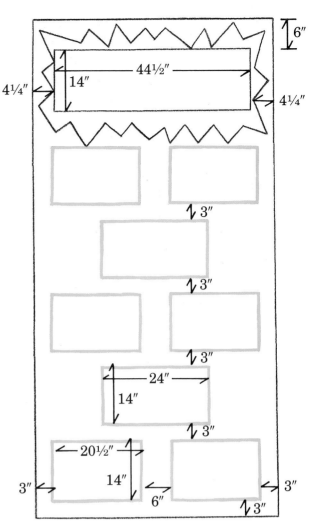

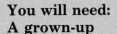

You will need:
A grown-up
53″ x 107″ piece of primed canvas
Pencil
Yardstick
Acrylic paints: green, blue, red, yellow,
    orange, purple
Paintbrushes
12″ stencils: numerals, letters
Masking tape
Clear acrylic sealer spray
Rubber toss piece

1. Place the canvas on a flat surface. Draw 2 (20½″-wide x 14″-high) rectangles at 1 short end of the canvas, spacing them 3″ from the edges of the canvas.

2. Using the diagram as a guide, center and draw a 24″-wide x 14″-high rectangle 3″ above the first 2 rectangles.

3. Repeat Steps 1 and 2 until you have 3 rows with 2 rectangles and 2 rows with 1 rectangle.

4. Using the diagram as a guide: Draw a 44½″-wide x 14″-high box 6″ from the top and 4¼″ from the edges of the canvas. Then draw large triangles around the box to create jagged edges. Draw geometric shapes on the mat as desired.

5. Outline the rectangles using the green paint. Let the paint dry.

23

6. Tape the corresponding numeral stencil in the center of each rectangle. Tape the letter stencils in the center of the jagged box to spell "HOME." Referring to the photo, paint the numerals and the letters as indicated. Let the paint dry. Remove the stencils. Paint the geometric shapes and the jagged box. Let the paint dry.

7. **Ask the grown-up** to spray the mat with the acrylic sealer.

Kringle Hop Rules

1. Standing on the opposite end of the mat from Home, players take turns throwing the toss piece. Once a player throws the toss piece, he or she must hop down the mat, (alternating 1 foot on every row with 1 rectangle), retrieve the toss piece, and then hop back.

2. Each player is awarded the number of points closest to where his or her toss piece lands. The rectangles are worth the number of points painted on them. Home is worth 10 points. If a player throws the piece off the mat, or if a player's foot lands outside of a rectangle, he or she loses 1 turn.

3. Each player gets 5 tosses. The player with the most points wins.

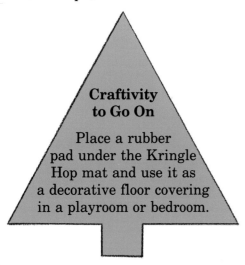

Craftivity to Go On

Place a rubber pad under the Kringle Hop mat and use it as a decorative floor covering in a playroom or bedroom.

24

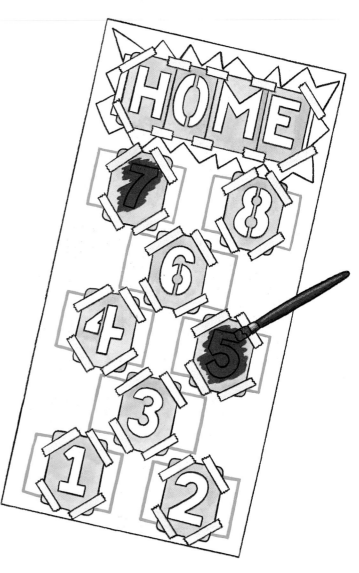

Friendship Ornaments

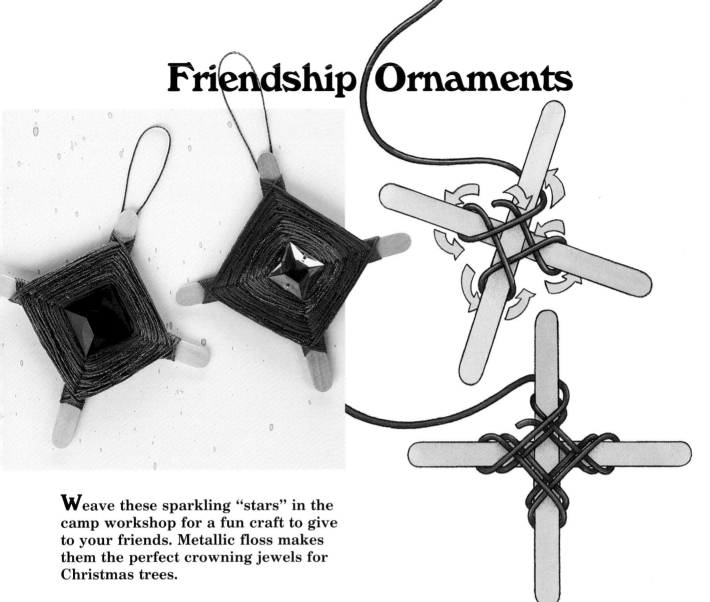

Weave these sparkling "stars" in the camp workshop for a fun craft to give to your friends. Metallic floss makes them the perfect crowning jewels for Christmas trees.

You will need (for 1 ornament):
2 wooden craft sticks
Tacky glue
DMC embroidery floss: purple #333, green #700
Kreinik metallic floss: purple #012HL, green #008
Scissors
¾" square acrylic jewel in desired color

1. Place 1 craft stick on top of the other, forming a cross. Glue the sticks together. Let the glue dry.

2. Handle 6 strands of the embroidery floss and 1 strand of the metallic floss of the same color as 1 unit. Wrap the floss over and around each stick, working clockwise as shown. Continue in this manner until the desired width of that color is achieved. Cut the floss and glue the ends to the back to secure. Repeat with the remaining color of floss, wrapping until the floss is ½" from the ends of each stick.

3. For the hanger, cut a 6" length in the desired color. Fold the length in half and glue the cut ends to the back of 1 stick.

Memory Book

You will need:
13½″ x 46″ piece of heavyweight green-
  and-white ticking
Straight pins
Water-soluble marker
Ruler
Large-eyed needle
1¾ yards of red yarn
Pinking shears
Hole punch
Card stock sheets: 15 (8½″ x 11″) black, 1
  (6½″ x 9″) white
1 (11″ x 12″) 3-ring binder
Glue
⅞ yard of red rickrack
Permanent black marker (optional)

Our campers show off their favorite camp photos and try their hands at simple sewing with a one-of-a-kind scrapbook. Just cover an old school notebook with fabric, accent it with running stitches, and you've got a special place to store your memorabilia from any occasion.

1. Place the fabric right side down on a flat surface.

2. With wrong sides facing, fold each short edge 10″ toward the center. Pin the fabric in place around the edges to form flaps.

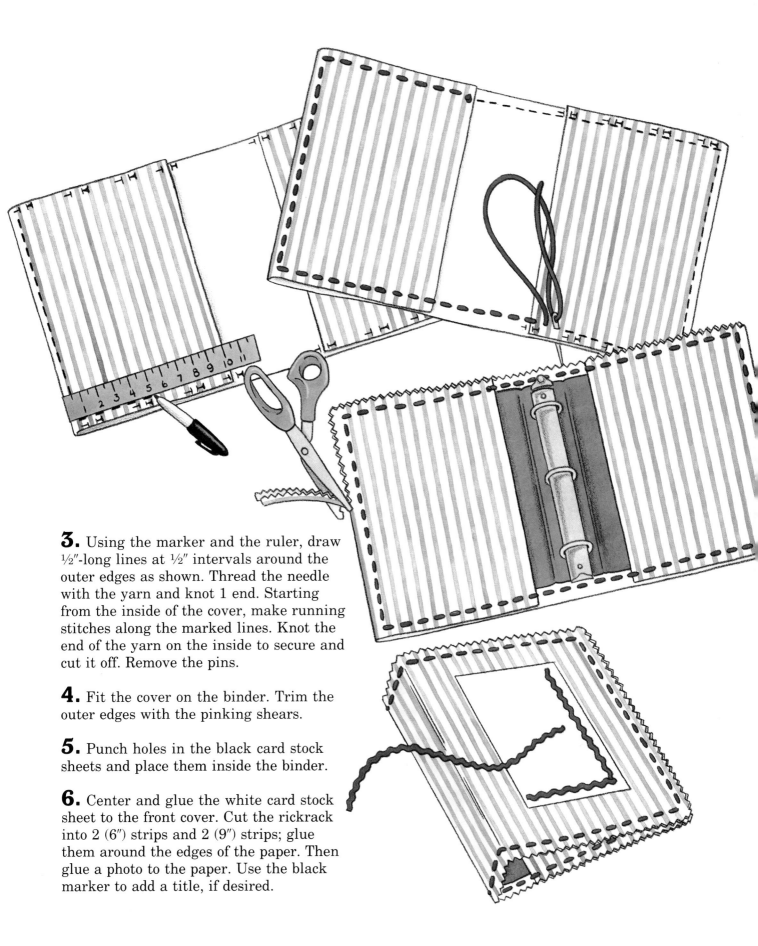

3. Using the marker and the ruler, draw ½"-long lines at ½" intervals around the outer edges as shown. Thread the needle with the yarn and knot 1 end. Starting from the inside of the cover, make running stitches along the marked lines. Knot the end of the yarn on the inside to secure and cut it off. Remove the pins.

4. Fit the cover on the binder. Trim the outer edges with the pinking shears.

5. Punch holes in the black card stock sheets and place them inside the binder.

6. Center and glue the white card stock sheet to the front cover. Cut the rickrack into 2 (6") strips and 2 (9") strips; glue them around the edges of the paper. Then glue a photo to the paper. Use the black marker to add a title, if desired.

Twig Tree

2. Wrap the remaining ribbon around the middle of the bow. Starting at the back of the bow, wrap it around to the front and over the top to the back again, leaving a long tail (see back view in diagram).

3. Using the paint pens, decorate some of the twigs. Use the photo as a guide or create your own designs.

4. Arrange the sticks on the ribbon tail, starting with the shortest beneath the bow and finishing with the longest. When you are satisfied with the arrangement of the twigs, glue them in place. For the tree trunk, glue a short, thick stick to the bottom of the ribbon tail. Let the glue dry for 24 hours.

5. Thread the elastic band through the bow and knot the ends to form a hanger.

Kids got sidetracked gathering wood for a campfire and ended up making these miniature trees instead. Take a nature walk and gather some twigs to make your own holiday decorations.

You will need (for 1 tree):
⅔ yard of red metallic ribbon
Scissors
Founder's Adhesive glue
1 clothespin
9–14 twigs, ranging in size from 6″ to 1″
Fine-point paint pens: gold, green, red
8″ piece of gold elastic band

1. Cut the ribbon in half. Fold 1 piece of the ribbon into the shape of a bow. Glue it together in the center and secure it with a clothespin. Let the glue dry.

Kringle Eats 'n' Treats

After a long day of activities, enjoy a steaming cup of Campfire Cocoa and some Chocolate-Covered Snowballs while you warm yourself by the fire.

Kringle Jingle has been busy in the kitchen whipping up lots of recipes for special holiday feasts. Turn the page and choose your favorite!

Children's Workshop
Happy Holiday Crafts

Lighten Up

Brighten any tree, mantel, staircase, or doorway with overgrown felt lights and rick-rack cording. These bulbs are fun to make and to string along.

You will need:

Green jumbo rickrack (See Step 1 for length.)
Tracing paper
Pencil
Scissors
Felt: black, assorted colors
Fabric glue
Large safety pin

1. Before you begin, decide where you want to hang your garland. Cut a strip of rickrack to fit this space. Then determine how many lights you will need to hang on your garland.

2. Trace and cut out the patterns. Trace the patterns onto the felt to make as many lights as desired. Cut them out.

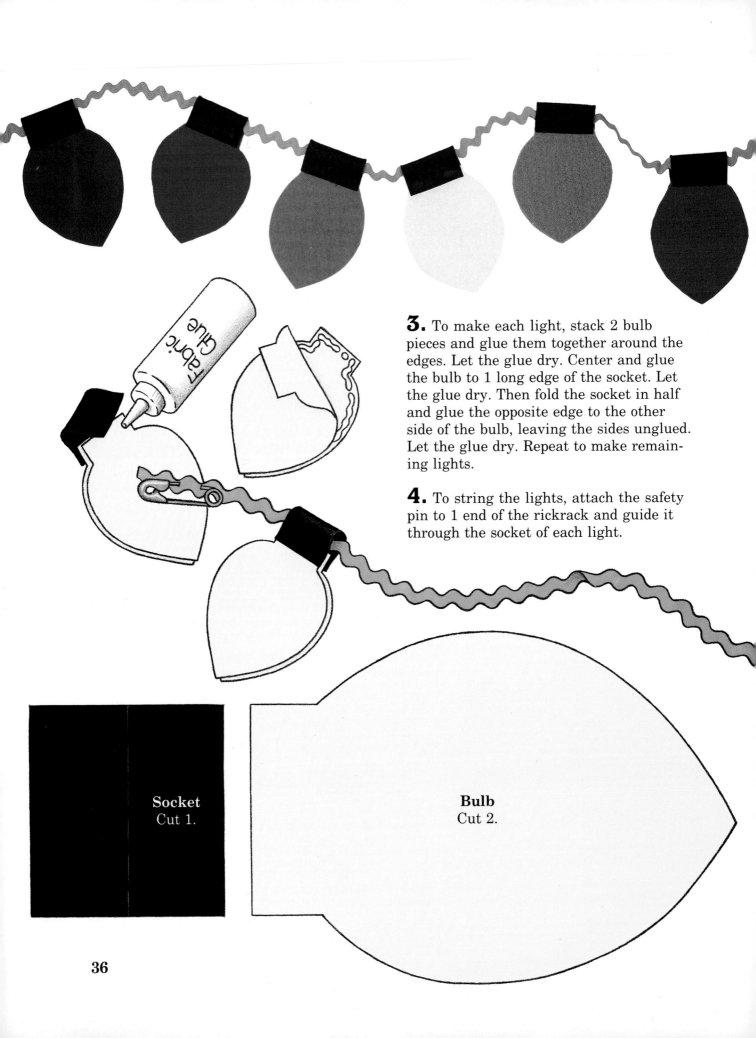

3. To make each light, stack 2 bulb pieces and glue them together around the edges. Let the glue dry. Center and glue the bulb to 1 long edge of the socket. Let the glue dry. Then fold the socket in half and glue the opposite edge to the other side of the bulb, leaving the sides unglued. Let the glue dry. Repeat to make remaining lights.

4. To string the lights, attach the safety pin to 1 end of the rickrack and guide it through the socket of each light.

Socket
Cut 1.

Bulb
Cut 2.

Bag It and Tag It

Need a quick idea for wrapping? Turn a colorful bag into a decorative hiding place for holiday surprises. Then top it off with a matching gift tag. Use our patterns—or make your own by tracing a favorite cookie cutter.

You will need (for each bag):
A grown-up
Tracing paper
Pencil
Scissors
Gift bag
Scrap of cardboard
Craft knife
1 sheet of clear acetate
Craft glue
Damp cloth
Hole punch
Colored marker
Scrap of ribbon to match bag

1. Trace and cut out the desired pattern. Transfer the pattern onto the bag as many times as desired.

2. Place the cardboard inside the bag to protect the back. **Ask the grown-up** to help you cut out each shape using the craft knife. Remove the cardboard and set the cutouts aside.

3. To cover the openings, place the acetate sheet over the cutout shapes. Mark a 1″ margin around the shapes and cut the acetate along these lines. Open the bag and apply the glue around the shapes on the inside of the bag. Place the acetate over the openings and press. Wipe away any excess glue with the damp cloth.

4. To make the gift tag, punch a hole in the top of 1 of the cutouts you set aside. Write your greetings on the back of the tag. Thread the ribbon through the hole and tie it around the handle of the bag.

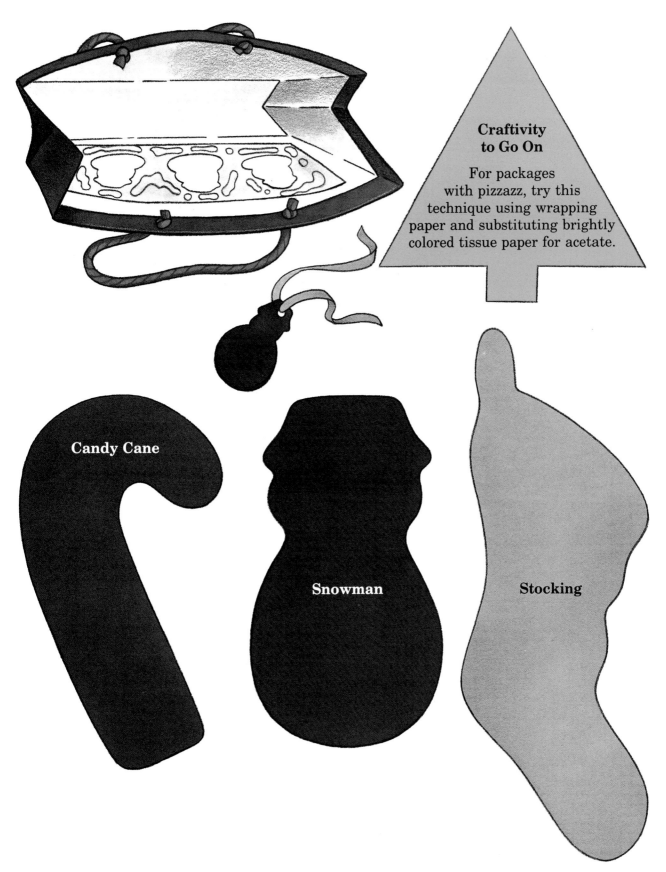

Craftivity to Go On

For packages with pizzazz, try this technique using wrapping paper and substituting brightly colored tissue paper for acetate.

Candy Cane

Snowman

Stocking

39

Pet Stockings

Include a furry friend in your celebration with a clever stocking. Then stuff it with surprises that come in small sizes!

You will need (for each stocking):
Tracing paper
Pencil
Scissors
Water-soluble marker
Fabric glue
1⅛ yards of yellow yarn
Large-eyed needle
¾ yard of thin pink paper cording
For the bone: ¼ yard of orange felt; scraps of red, yellow, pink, and green felt; ¾ yard (1″-wide) green polka-dot ribbon
For the mouse: ¼ yard of red felt, scraps of pink and blue felt, ⅝ yard (⅛″-wide) blue satin ribbon, ¾ yard (1″-wide) blue polka-dot ribbon

Note: For a stocking stuffer, see Crunchy Pet Cookies on pages 86–88.

1. Trace and cut out the desired stocking pattern, marking the stitching lines. Trace the pattern onto the felt 2 times. Cut out the pieces. Using the water-soluble marker, transfer the stitching lines to 1 stocking piece. **For the mouse:** Also transfer stitching lines to each leg piece.

Trace and cut out the details. Trace the details onto the color of felt indicated and cut them out. Set the details aside.

2. For the mouse: Glue the feet to 1 side of the unmarked stocking piece (see pattern for placement). Cut small slits in the feet to make the toes. Referring to the photo, glue the outside edge of each leg to the remaining stocking piece, aligning the marked stitching lines. Let the glue dry. Thread the needle with the yarn and knot 1 end. Using the yellow yarn and a running stitch, sew each leg to the stocking front along the **inside edge only.** Then stitch the 2 center stitches to finish the legs (see photo). Knot the thread to secure and cut it off.

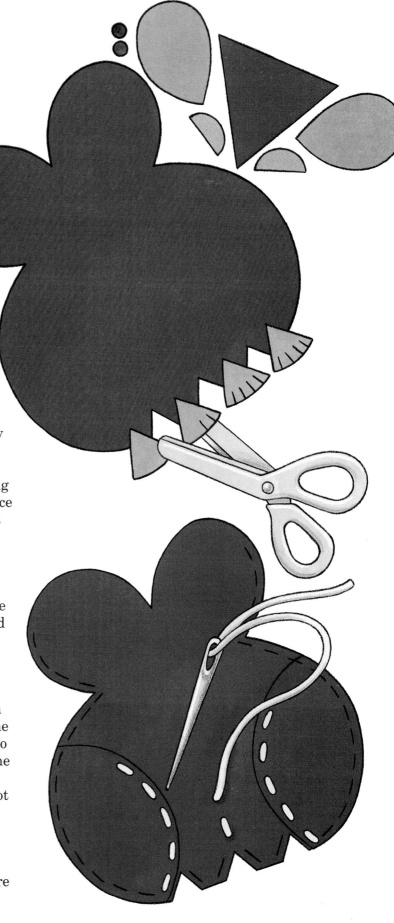

Level 3

3. Place the stocking front faceup on the stocking back, aligning the edges. Thread the needle with the yarn and knot 1 end. Using the yellow yarn and a running stitch, sew the stocking pieces together, following the marked stitching lines. Knot the thread to secure and cut it off.

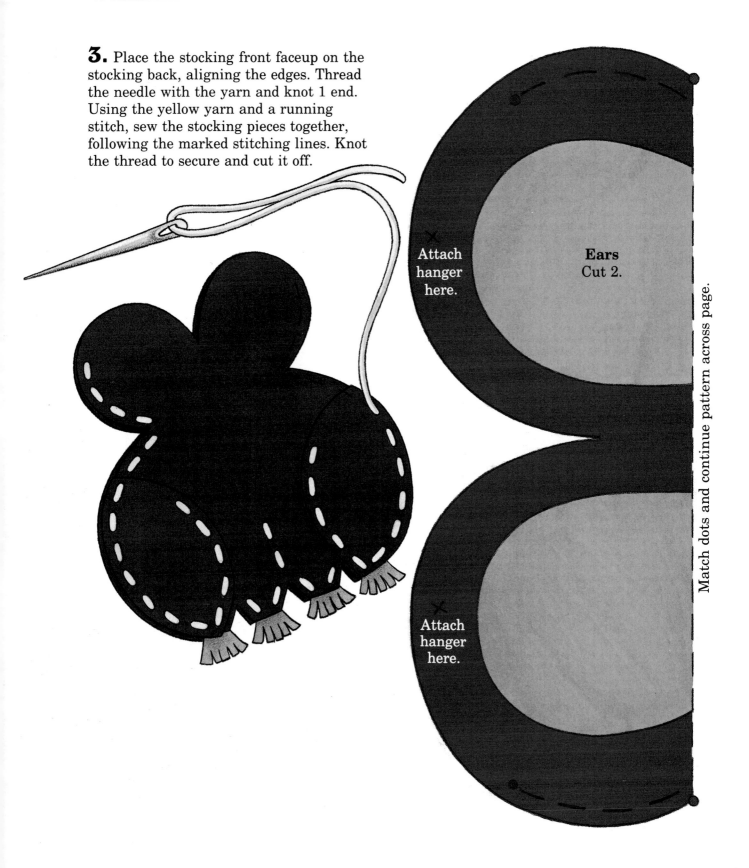

Attach hanger here.

Ears
Cut 2.

Attach hanger here.

Match dots and continue pattern across page.

42

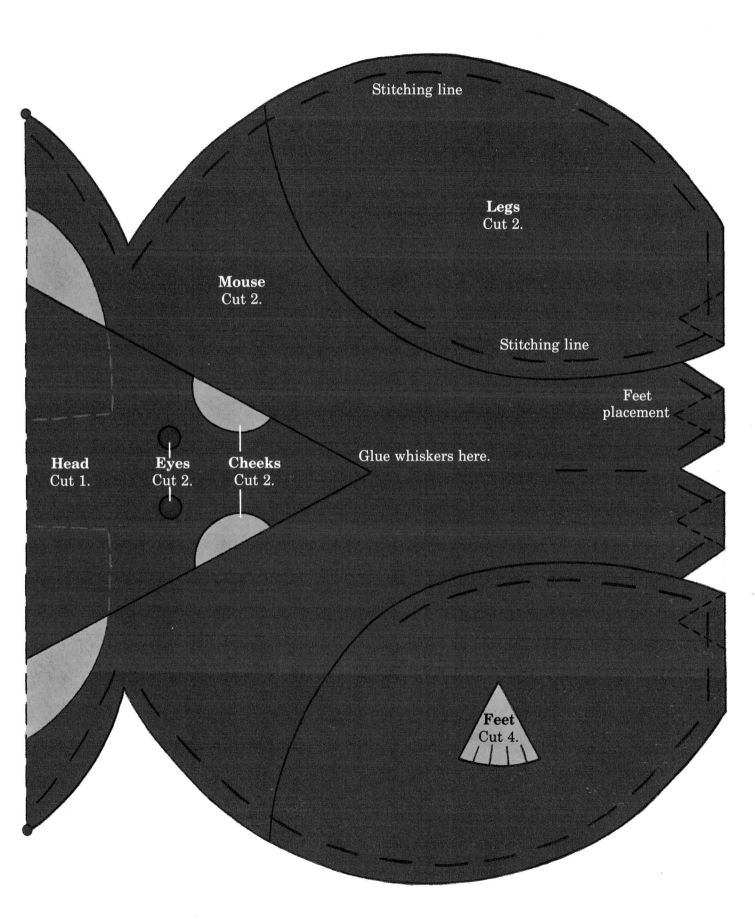

Stitching line

Legs
Cut 2.

Stitching line

Feet
placement

Mouse
Cut 2.

Head
Cut 1.

Eyes
Cut 2.

Cheeks
Cut 2.

Glue whiskers here.

Feet
Cut 4.

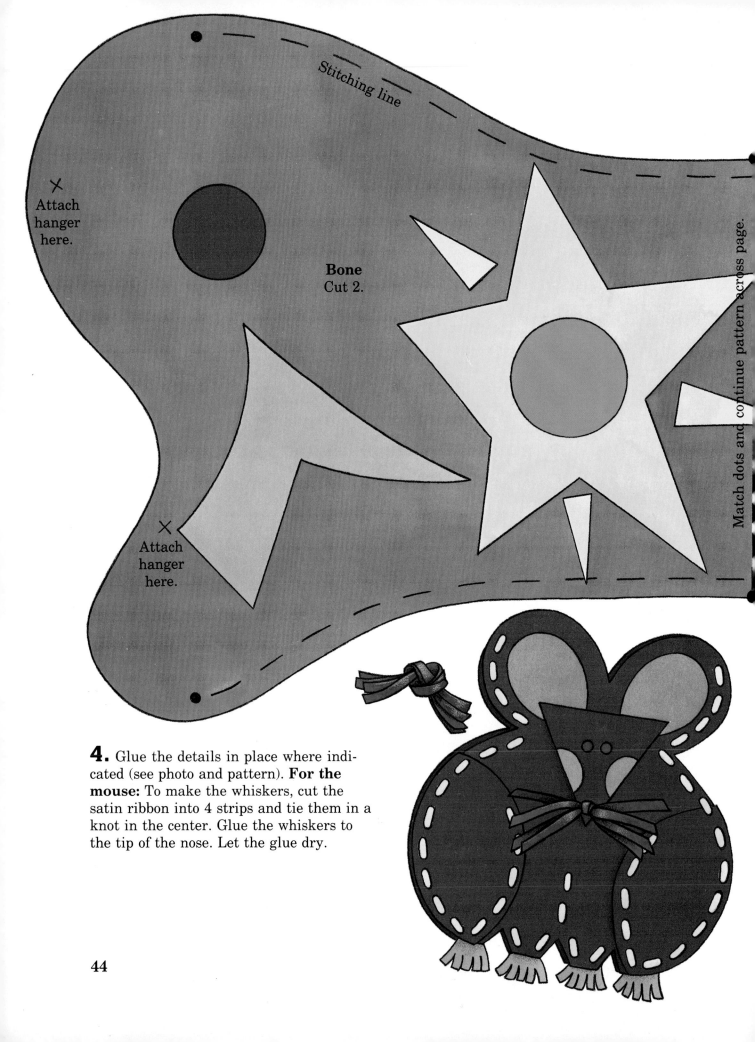

Attach hanger here. ✕

Attach hanger here. ✕

Stitching line

Bone
Cut 2.

Match dots and continue pattern across page.

4. Glue the details in place where indicated (see photo and pattern). **For the mouse:** To make the whiskers, cut the satin ribbon into 4 strips and tie them in a knot in the center. Glue the whiskers to the tip of the nose. Let the glue dry.

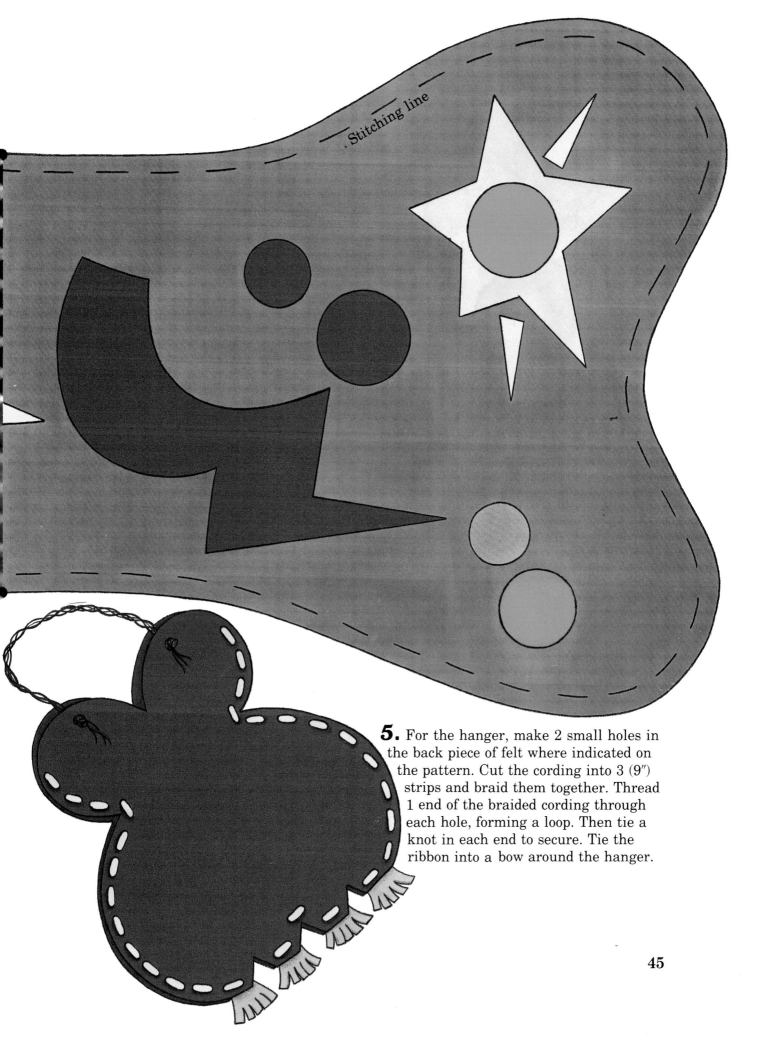

Stitching line

5. For the hanger, make 2 small holes in the back piece of felt where indicated on the pattern. Cut the cording into 3 (9″) strips and braid them together. Thread 1 end of the braided cording through each hole, forming a loop. Then tie a knot in each end to secure. Tie the ribbon into a bow around the hanger.

45

Clearly Christmas Banners

If it doesn't snow in your town this Christmas, stick one of these banners to a window or a glass door and make it look as if it's snowing ornaments or—even more likely—snowflakes!

You will need (for each banner):
Tracing paper
Pencil
7″ x 23″ piece of clear vinyl
Paint pens in assorted colors
Damp sponge

1. Trace the desired pattern.

2. Place the traced pattern on a flat surface. Beginning at the left edge, place the vinyl strip over the traced pattern.

3. Using the desired colors, paint the design onto the banner. Let the paint dry. Slide the pattern to the right, tilt it in a different direction, and paint the design. Let the paint dry. Continue in this manner until the banner is full.

4. When the banner is completely dry, wet the unpainted side of the plastic with the damp sponge and stick it to a window or a glass door. Carefully smooth any wrinkles with your hand.

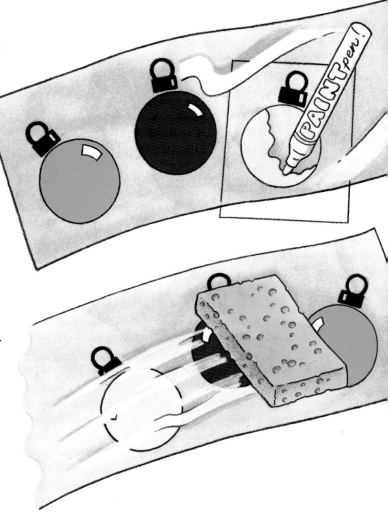

Color Melts

Hold these ornaments up to a sunny window and watch the light filter through them. Their translucent appearance resembles stained glass but actually comes from crayon shavings melted between waxed paper.

You will need (for each ornament):
A grown-up
Tracing paper
Pencil
Scissors
Heavyweight colored paper
Masking tape
Waxed paper
Ironing board
2 cloth towels
Crayons in desired colors
Vegetable peeler
Iron
Glue
Hole punch
Scrap of satin ribbon

1. Trace and cut out the desired pattern. Fold the heavyweight paper in half and trace the pattern onto the paper.

2. Tape the 2 layers of the paper together to hold them in place. Cut along the inner and the outer edges of the design. Set the 2 shapes aside.

3. Repeat Steps 1 and 2 with the waxed paper, cutting along the **outer** edge only. Do not tape the layers together.

4. Cover the ironing board with 1 towel. Place 1 waxed paper cutout on the cloth. Remove the paper from the crayons. Using the peeler, shave different colored crayons onto the waxed paper, lightly covering the surface. (Be careful not to make a pile of shavings or your ornament will appear dark.)

Aligning the edges, place the remaining waxed paper cutout on top of the first, sandwiching the shavings in between. Place the remaining towel on top of the waxed paper and **ask the grown-up** to lightly press the 2 layers with a warm iron until the shavings are melted. Let the waxed paper cool.

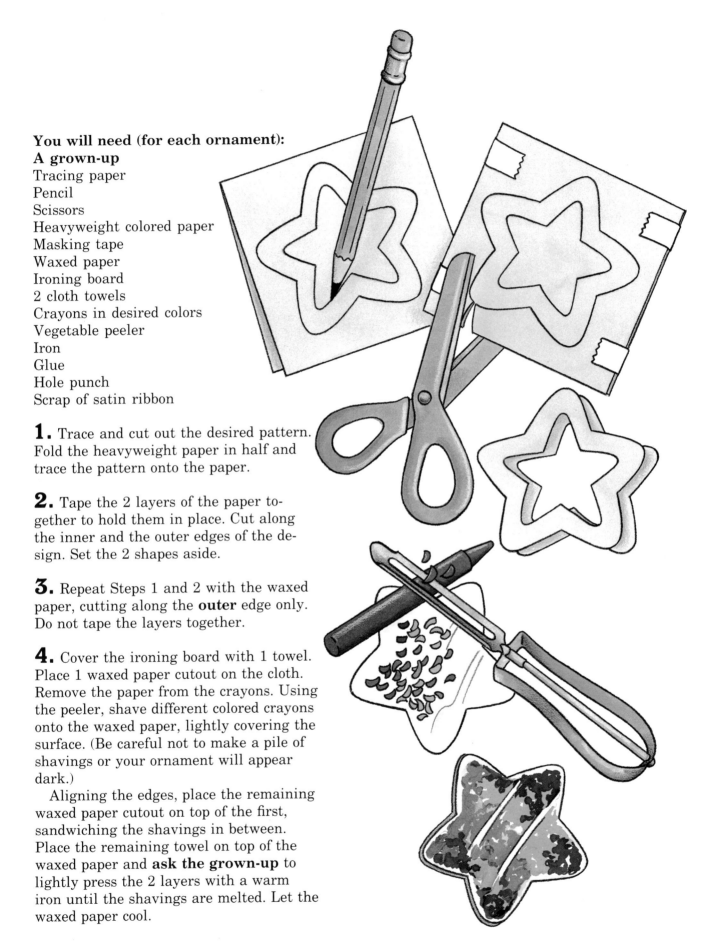

5. Sandwich the waxed paper pieces between the 2 heavyweight paper shapes, aligning the edges. (Trim any excess waxed paper around the edges of the ornament.) Glue the layers together along the outer edges. Let the glue dry.

6. Using the hole punch, make a hole in the ornament where indicated.

7. For the hanger, thread the ribbon through the hole and tie the ends together in a knot.

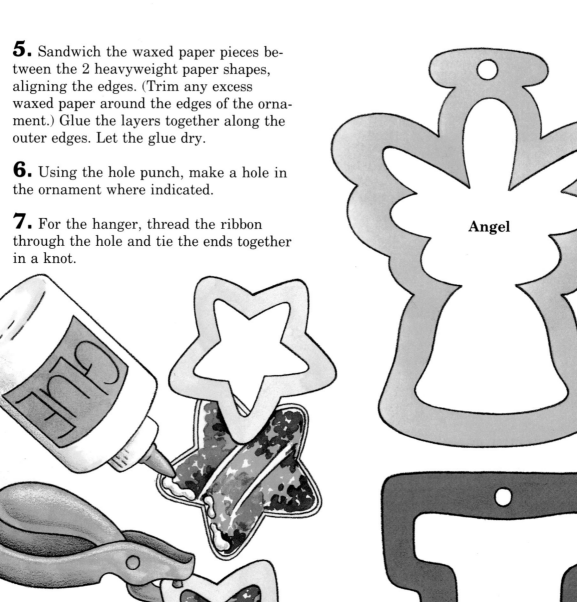

Angel

Stocking

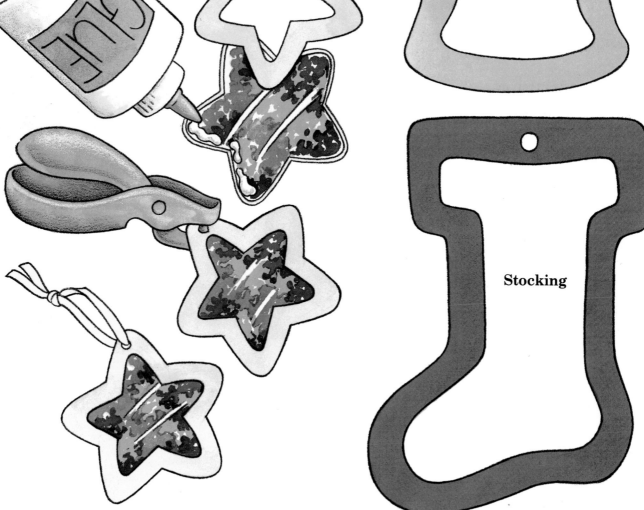

Star

Tree

Bell

Bird

Candy Cane

51

Greetings from Toyland

Hand in hand, these holiday cards are ready to deliver your Christmas wishes—they'll even stand up to do it! Write your greetings on the inside and send them on their merry way.

You will need (for each card):
Tracing paper
Pencil
Scissors
8½″ x 11″ sheet of white heavyweight paper
Fine-point black marker
Glue
Scraps of felt: red, green, yellow
Glitter: green, gold
Standard card envelope
For the ballerinas: 8½″ x 11″ sheet of pink heavyweight paper, fine-point pink marker, scraps of brown and pink felt, 6″ (⅛″-wide) red satin ribbon, scrap of red netting
For the nutcrackers: scrap of heavyweight pink paper, fine-point red marker, scraps of blue and orange felt

Ballerina Card

1. Trace and cut out the patterns.

2. Fold the white paper in half widthwise. Place the body pattern on the paper, aligning each head with the folded edge. Cut around the **outer edges** of the pattern so that the arms and the feet stick out from the card. Do not cut the top fold.

3. Trace the body pattern onto the pink paper and cut around the shapes, leaving the hands connected in the center.

4. Place the pink cutout on top of the card, aligning the arms and the feet. Glue the cutout in place. Let the glue dry.

5. Using the markers, draw the faces and add the details to the legs as shown on the pattern.

6. Trace the patterns onto the felt and then cut them out as follows: 2 hair pieces from the brown, 2 bows from the pink, 2 dresses and 4 pointe shoes from the red, 1 tree from the green, and 1 star from the yellow.

7. Referring to the photo: Glue the hair pieces around the face. Glue the bows to the hair. Glue 1 dress in the center of each body. Cut the satin ribbon into 8 (¾″) strips; glue 2 pieces in the shape of an X to each foot. Glue the pointe shoes at the tips of the feet, covering the ends of the ribbons. Let the glue dry.

Cover 1 side each of the tree and the star with glue. Sprinkle the tree with green glitter and the star with gold glitter. Glue the tree and the star in place as shown. Let the glue dry.

8. Cut 2 (2″ x 3″) pieces of netting. Gather each piece along 1 long edge. To form the tutus, glue the netting over the skirts along the gathered edges.

Nutcracker Card

1. Follow Steps 1 and 2 for the Ballerina Card.

2. Trace the face onto the pink paper 2 times; trace the inner hands and each outer hand once. Cut them out. Glue the faces and the hands in place as indicated on the pattern.

3. Using the markers, draw the faces as shown on the pattern.

4. Trace the patterns onto the felt and then cut them out as follows: 4 shoes and 2 shirts from the blue; 2 pairs of pants, 2 hats, and 2 bow ties from the red; 2 hair pieces, 2 ovals, 4 shoulder pieces, and 1 star from the yellow; 2 hatbands from the orange; and 1 tree from the green. Cut along the center of each pants piece.

5. Referring to the photo, glue the pieces in place as follows: the shoes, the pants, the shirts, the hair, the hats, the ovals, and the hatbands.

Cover 1 side each of the tree, the star, and the shoulder pieces with glue. Sprinkle the tree and 2 shoulder pieces with green glitter and the star and 2 shoulder pieces with gold glitter. Glue the tree and the star in place as shown. Glue 1 shoulder piece at the top of each shoulder. Glue 1 bow tie to the center top of each shirt. Let the glue dry.

55

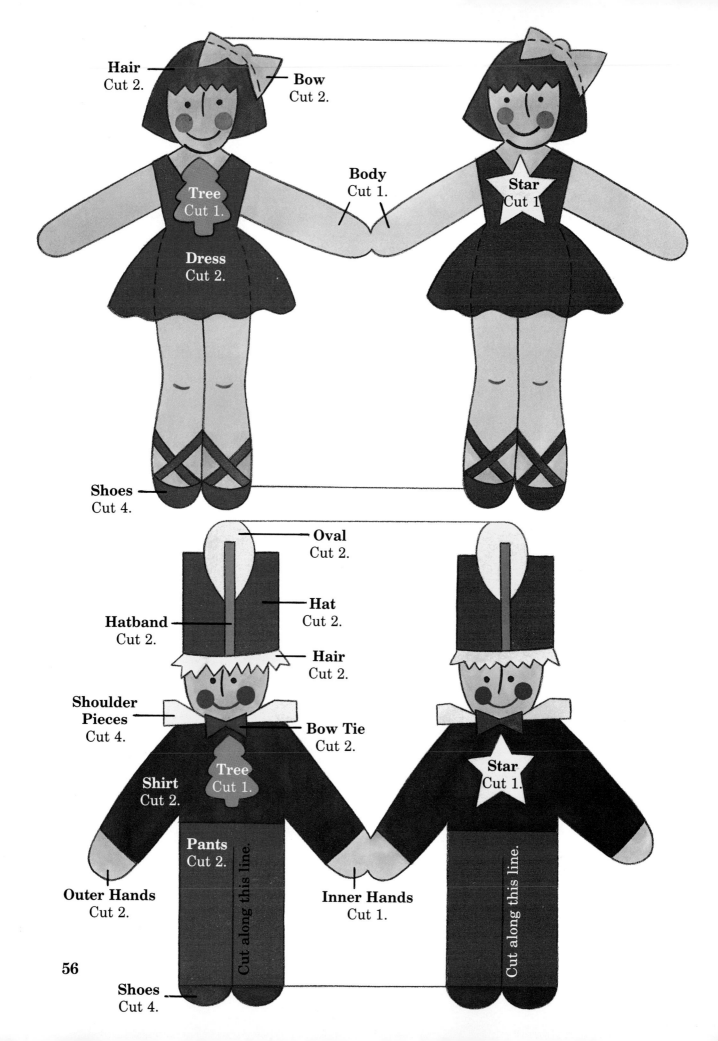

Hair Cut 2.

Bow Cut 2.

Tree Cut 1.

Body Cut 1.

Star Cut 1

Dress Cut 2.

Shoes Cut 4.

Oval Cut 2.

Hatband Cut 2.

Hat Cut 2.

Hair Cut 2.

Shoulder Pieces Cut 4.

Bow Tie Cut 2.

Shirt Cut 2.

Tree Cut 1.

Star Cut 1.

Outer Hands Cut 2.

Pants Cut 2.

Cut along this line.

Inner Hands Cut 1.

Cut along this line.

56

Shoes Cut 4.

Pop Goes the Snowman

Make this frosty figure for a centerpiece that won't melt when the sun comes out. Simply cover balloons with glue-coated string, let them dry, and pop the balloons to leave airy "snowballs."

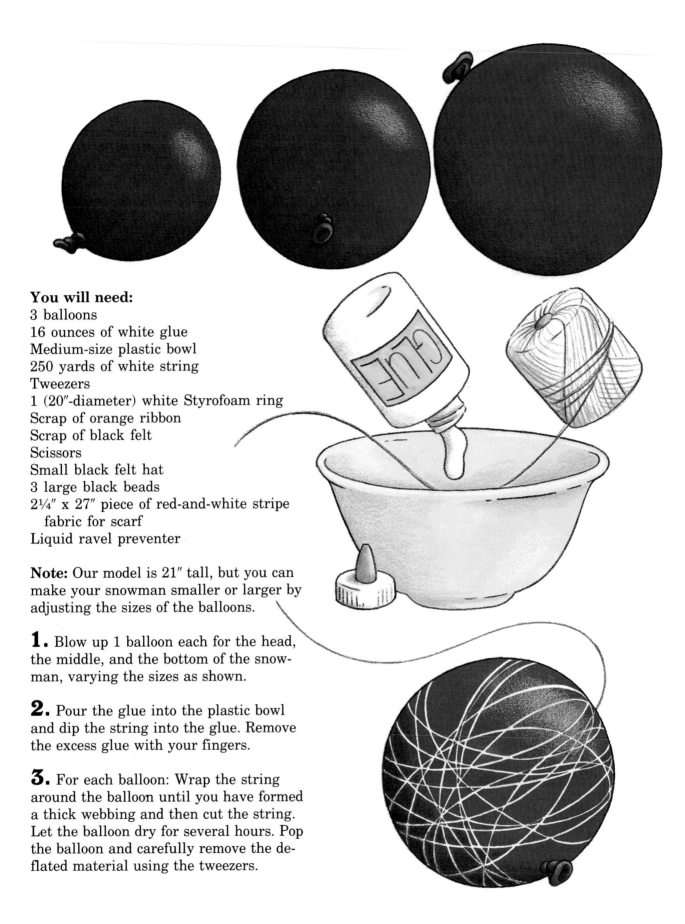

You will need:
3 balloons
16 ounces of white glue
Medium-size plastic bowl
250 yards of white string
Tweezers
1 (20″-diameter) white Styrofoam ring
Scrap of orange ribbon
Scrap of black felt
Scissors
Small black felt hat
3 large black beads
2¼″ x 27″ piece of red-and-white stripe
  fabric for scarf
Liquid ravel preventer

Note: Our model is 21″ tall, but you can make your snowman smaller or larger by adjusting the sizes of the balloons.

1. Blow up 1 balloon each for the head, the middle, and the bottom of the snowman, varying the sizes as shown.

2. Pour the glue into the plastic bowl and dip the string into the glue. Remove the excess glue with your fingers.

3. For each balloon: Wrap the string around the balloon until you have formed a thick webbing and then cut the string. Let the balloon dry for several hours. Pop the balloon and carefully remove the deflated material using the tweezers.

58

4. Glue the head, the middle, and the bottom together to form the body. Glue the bottom of the snowman in the center of the Styrofoam ring. Let the glue dry.

5. To make the nose, roll the orange ribbon into a cone shape and glue the ends together. Glue the nose in the center of the top balloon.

6. From the black felt, cut out 2 large circles for the eyes and 6 small circles for the mouth. Glue the eyes and the mouth in place on the top balloon. Glue the hat onto the top of the snowman's head.

7. Glue the beads in a straight line down the center of the middle balloon.

8. Apply a light coat of liquid ravel preventer to the long edges of the red-and-white stripe strip. To make fringe, cut tiny slits in each short edge. Wrap the scarf around the snowman's neck and tie it in place.

Fun Foam Forest

You won't need a ladder to trim these trees! And you can choose all the decorations yourself. Make one tree or a whole forest for a festive Christmas centerpiece.

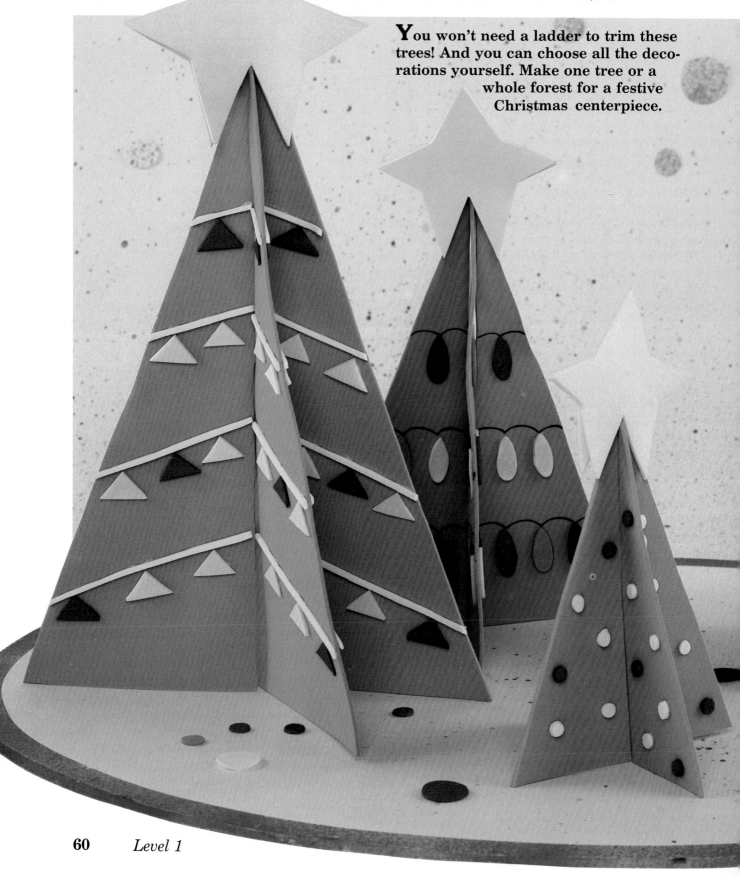

You will need (for each tree):
Tracing paper
Pencil
Scissors
Fun Foam: green, yellow, blue, black, red,
    orange, white
Founder's Adhesive glue
Water-soluble marker
Ruler
Hole punch (optional)
For the teardrop lights tree: fine-point
    permanent black marker

1. Decide which size tree you want to
make—small, medium, or large. Trace and
cut out the desired tree and star patterns.
Trace the patterns 2 times onto the color
foam indicated. Cut them out, making
sure to mark the bottom center on each
triangle.

2. To make the star, glue the 2 pieces
together along the outside edges, leaving
the bottom unglued. Set the star aside.

3. Using the water-soluble marker and the ruler, draw a straight line from the peak of the tree to the bottom center on 1 side of each triangle. Mark the center point of the tree on each line. On 1 triangle, cut along the marked line from the peak to the center point. On the other triangle, cut along the marked line from the bottom to the center point.

4. Referring to the photo, cut the decorations from assorted colors of foam and glue them to the triangles as desired. (Use the hole punch to make small circles.) **For the teardrop lights tree:** Referring to the photo and using the marker, draw scalloped lines on the front and the back of each triangle. Glue 1 teardrop at the tip of each scallop. Let the glue dry.

5. To form the tree, slide the triangle with the slit at the bottom into the triangle with the slit at the top. Place the star on top of the tree so that the top edges of the tree fit inside.

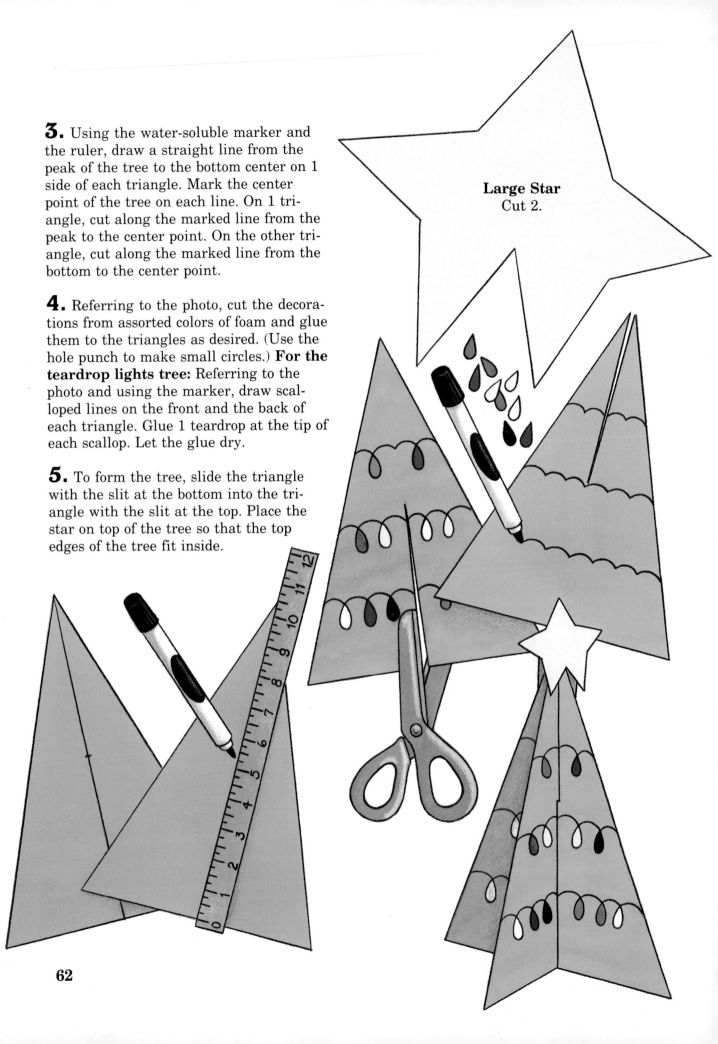

Large Star
Cut 2.

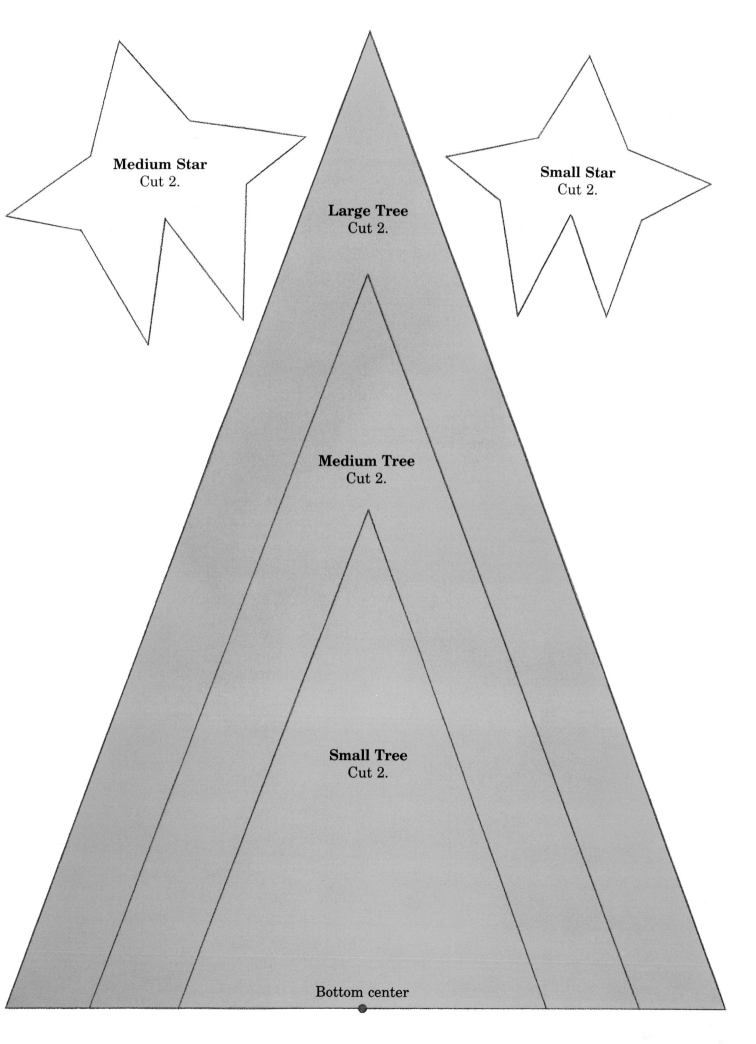

Medium Star
Cut 2.

Small Star
Cut 2.

Large Tree
Cut 2.

Medium Tree
Cut 2.

Small Tree
Cut 2.

Bottom center

Make an Impression

The shiny background of these post-cards looks like metal, but it's really household foil. Draw a winter scene and create your own unique Christmas postcard. Just let your imagination be your guide.

You will need (for each card):
Newspaper
4″ x 6″ piece of heavy-duty aluminum foil
Dull pencil
Black ink
Paintbrush
Paper towel
Glue
4½″ x 6½″ piece of colored mat board
Permanent marker

1. Fold several sheets of newspaper to make a padded work surface.

2. Place the foil on the newspaper. Using the dull pencil, draw a design.

3. Paint 1 coat of black ink over the drawing. Using the paper towel, gently wipe off the excess ink. Let the ink dry.

4. Glue the foil in the center of the mat board. Write your greeting on the back of the postcard.

It's a Stick Up!

Give ordinary boxes personality plus by
decorating with colorful stickers, rickrack,
and ribbon. These packages are sure to
bring smiles on Christmas Day—even
before the gifts
inside are
revealed!

You will need (for each box):
Scissors
Liquid ravel preventer
Glue

For the automobile box: red rectangular box, 1″-wide black-and-white stripe grosgrain ribbon, assorted automobile and party hat stickers

For the face box: small pink round box, 8″ piece of ⅜″-wide pink grosgrain ribbon, 8″ piece and scrap of ⅜″-wide yellow grosgrain ribbon, ½ yard (1½″-wide) pink-and-white polka-dot grosgrain ribbon, scrap of ¾″-wide pink grosgrain ribbon, 2 small and 1 large pink heart stickers, 1 small and 2 large red circle stickers

For the tree box: white square box, large tree sticker, scraps of ¼″-wide yellow rickrack, assorted star and ornament stickers, ½ yard (⅜″-wide) red-and-white polka-dot grosgrain ribbon

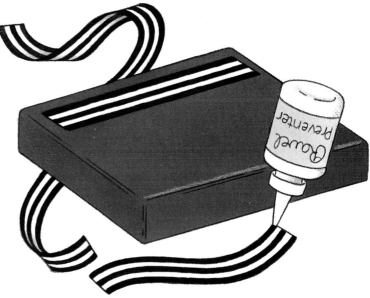

Automobile Box

1. Before you begin, measure across the top and the bottom of the box to determine how much ribbon you will need. Cut the ribbon into 2 strips to fit. Apply liquid ravel preventer to the cut ends of the ribbon and glue 1 strip each along the top and the bottom edges of the box top.

2. Place the automobile stickers between the ribbon strips. Add the hat stickers as desired.

Face Box

1. To make the hair, apply liquid ravel preventer to the ends of the ⅜″-wide pink and yellow ribbon pieces. Handling both strips as 1 unit, glue the center of the ribbons to the box at the center top. Twist the ribbons along each side to make curls and glue them in place at the edges of the box top (see photo).

2. Tie the polka-dot ribbon into a large bow and cut off the tails. Wrap the pink ribbon scrap around the center of the bow and glue it in place. Wrap the yellow ribbon scrap around the center of the pink ribbon and glue it in place. Glue the bow in the center of the hair.

3. To make the face, apply 2 small heart stickers for the eyes, 1 large heart sticker for the mouth, 1 small circle sticker for the nose, and 2 large circle stickers for the cheeks (see photo).

Tree Box

1. Center and apply the tree sticker diagonally on the box top.

2. Cut the rickrack into 2 strips, slightly longer than the width of the tree. Glue them across the tree (see photo).

3. Decorate the tree with the star and the ornament stickers as desired. Arrange the remaining stars around the tree as desired.

4. Tie the ribbon into a bow and glue it to the top of the tree.

Santa's Welcome Mat

Greet your holiday guests and Santa himself with a jolly ho, ho, ho! Mom and Dad will love this finger-painted mat because everyone will remember to wipe his or her feet at the door.

You will need:
A grown-up
27″ x 22½″ piece of raw canvas
Iron
Fabric glue
Tracing paper
Pencil
Scissors
Fabric paints: red, green, gold
3 paper plates
Clear acrylic sealer spray

1. With the wrong side of the canvas facing up, **ask the grown-up** to fold and press the canvas with a warm iron as follows: Fold each corner toward the center as shown. Press. Fold the side edges 1″ to the back as shown. Press. Repeat for the bottom edges.

2. Glue all folds in place. Let the glue dry. Turn the canvas right side up.

3. Trace and cut out the pattern. Beginning in the lower right corner, trace the letters onto the canvas. Then move the pattern slightly up and to the left; trace the letters again. Repeat.

4. Pour each color of paint onto a separate plate. Refer to the photo for placement of the trees and the presents. Wash and dry your finger or your thumb before changing colors.

Using your index finger: Paint the letters red. Paint each tree green, moving your finger from side to side in short strokes. Paint a gold dot at the top of each tree.

Using your thumb, paint the base of each tree red. For each present, use desired colors and paint a cross using your finger, 4 blocks around each cross using your thumb, and a V shape at the center top for the bow using your index finger. Repeat as desired. Let the paint dry.

5. **Ask the grown-up** to spray the entire mat with the acrylic sealer.

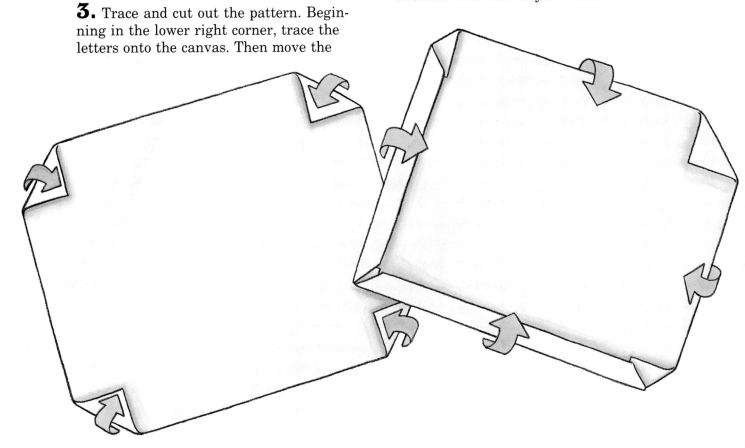

71

Napkin Appliqué Planter

Give an ordinary basket a face-lift and turn it into a colorful planter for Mom by using this easy paper napkin appliqué technique. Simply select napkins with distinct patterns and bright colors—then start cutting!

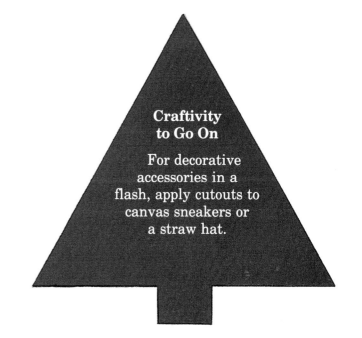

You will need:
Scissors
Decorative paper napkins to match basket
Aleene's Paper Napkin Appliqué™ Glue
Paper plate
Paintbrush
Natural or colored basket

1. Cut out enough designs from the napkins to decorate your basket as desired. For each design, remove the bottom layers of the napkin, leaving 1 ply.

2. Pour the glue onto the paper plate. Arranging the cutouts on the basket 1 at a time, use the paintbrush and the glue to lightly coat the area where you wish to place a cutout. Press the cutout onto the glue, smoothing the edges. Then lightly coat the front of the cutout with glue. Allow the glue to dry for several hours.

3. Fill the basket with a potted plant. Decorate the plant if desired.

Craftivity to Go On

For decorative accessories in a flash, apply cutouts to canvas sneakers or a straw hat.

Coupon Catalog

Good for 1...

CAR WASH

CLOSET CLEANED

These coupons are special because they can only be redeemed at home. Fill your catalog with chores like washing the car, taking out the trash, or feeding a pet.

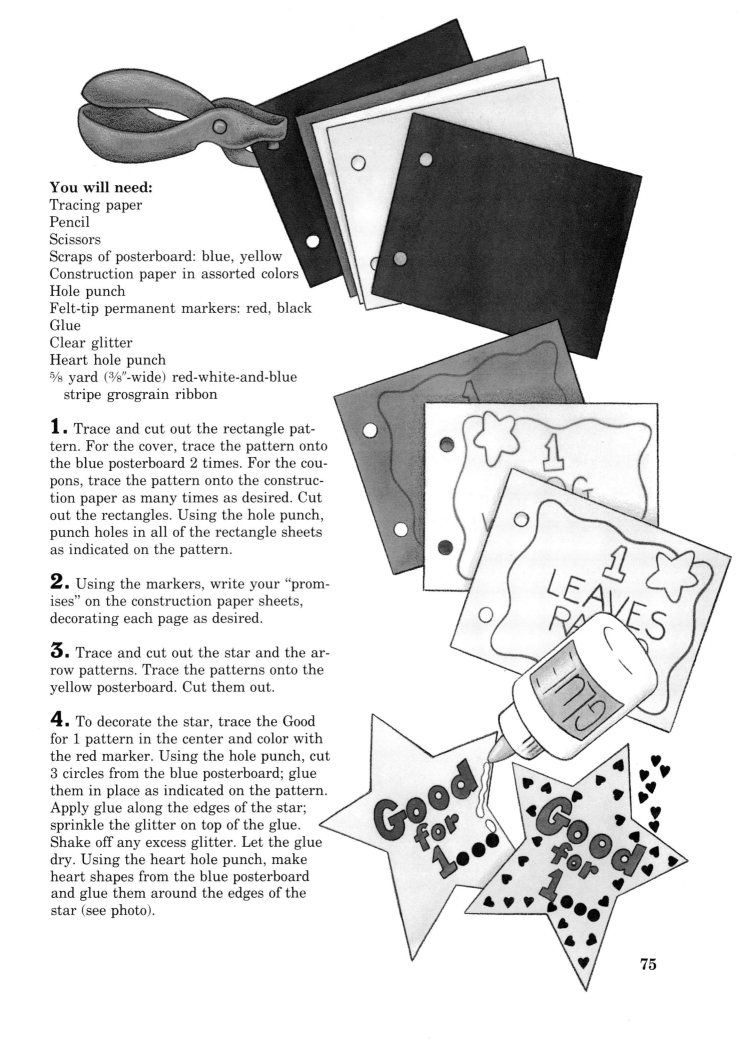

You will need:
Tracing paper
Pencil
Scissors
Scraps of posterboard: blue, yellow
Construction paper in assorted colors
Hole punch
Felt-tip permanent markers: red, black
Glue
Clear glitter
Heart hole punch
⅝ yard (⅜"-wide) red-white-and-blue
　　stripe grosgrain ribbon

1. Trace and cut out the rectangle pattern. For the cover, trace the pattern onto the blue posterboard 2 times. For the coupons, trace the pattern onto the construction paper as many times as desired. Cut out the rectangles. Using the hole punch, punch holes in all of the rectangle sheets as indicated on the pattern.

2. Using the markers, write your "promises" on the construction paper sheets, decorating each page as desired.

3. Trace and cut out the star and the arrow patterns. Trace the patterns onto the yellow posterboard. Cut them out.

4. To decorate the star, trace the Good for 1 pattern in the center and color with the red marker. Using the hole punch, cut 3 circles from the blue posterboard; glue them in place as indicated on the pattern. Apply glue along the edges of the star; sprinkle the glitter on top of the glue. Shake off any excess glitter. Let the glue dry. Using the heart hole punch, make heart shapes from the blue posterboard and glue them around the edges of the star (see photo).

5. Glue the star to 1 piece of the blue posterboard. Glue the yellow arrow in place as indicated on the pattern.

6. Place the construction paper sheets between the 2 posterboard sheets with the star on top. Thread the ribbon through the holes and tie it into a bow.

76

Something's Fishy

Fish soup, anyone? These whimsical place mats will make any meal a fun feast. And they're sure to bring out the seafood-lover in anyone on your gift list.

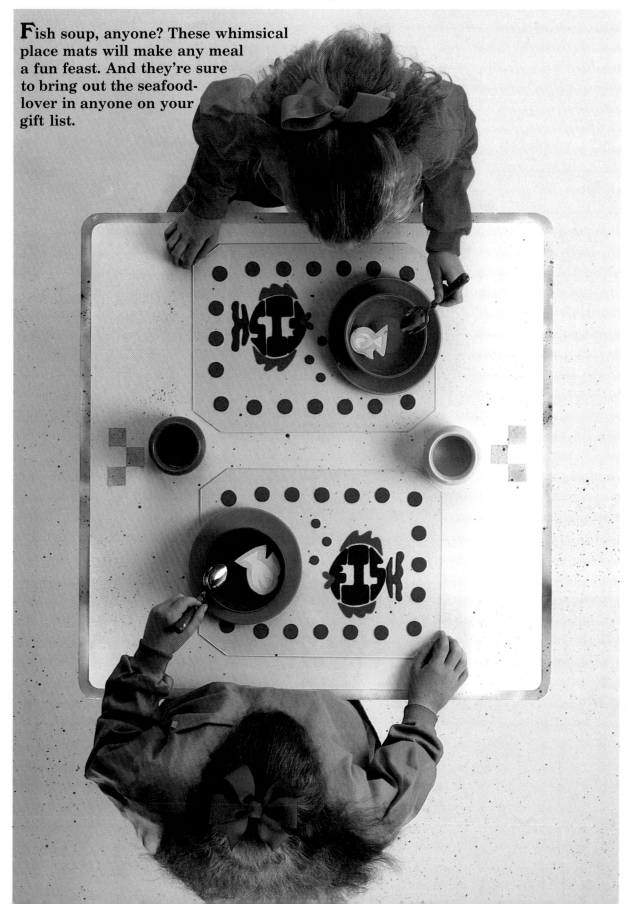

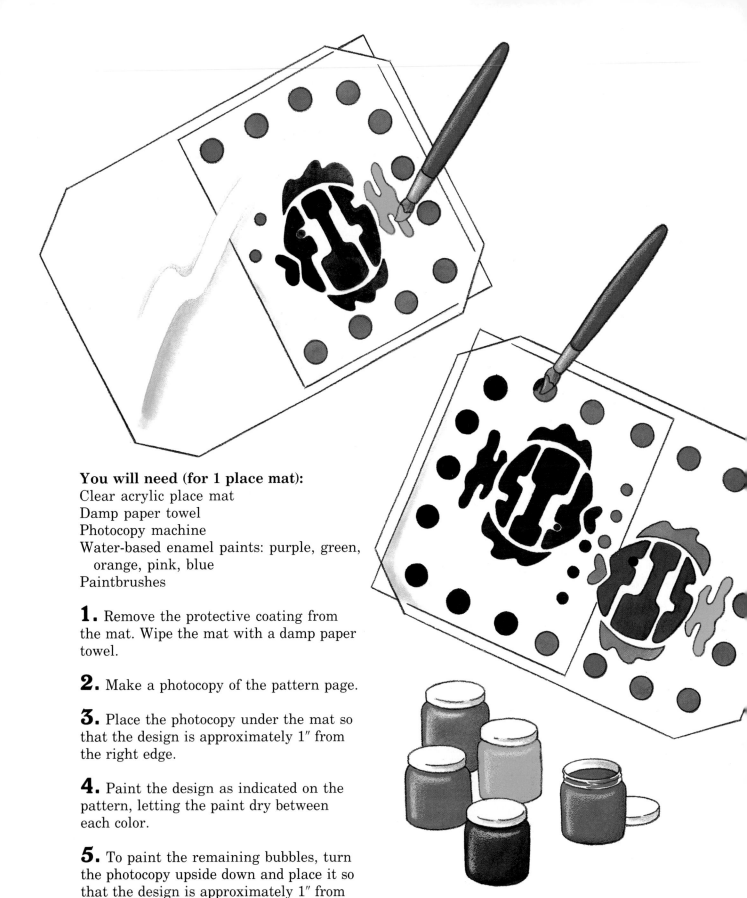

You will need (for 1 place mat):
Clear acrylic place mat
Damp paper towel
Photocopy machine
Water-based enamel paints: purple, green,
    orange, pink, blue
Paintbrushes

1. Remove the protective coating from
the mat. Wipe the mat with a damp paper
towel.

2. Make a photocopy of the pattern page.

3. Place the photocopy under the mat so
that the design is approximately 1″ from
the right edge.

4. Paint the design as indicated on the
pattern, letting the paint dry between
each color.

5. To paint the remaining bubbles, turn
the photocopy upside down and place it so
that the design is approximately 1″ from
the left edge. Paint the bubbles. Let the
place mat dry for several hours.

79

Oh, Deer!

On, Dasher! On, Dancer! On, Prancer and Vixen! Onto your sweater, that is. Make snazzy reindeer pins with wild and crazy details to wear throughout the holiday season.

You will need (for 1 pin):
Tracing paper
Pencil
Scissors
Heavyweight watercolor paper
Founder's Adhesive glue
Paintbrushes
Gesso
Acrylic paints in assorted colors
Fine-tip permanent black marker
Pin back

1. Trace and cut out the pattern. Transfer the pattern onto the heavyweight paper 2 times. Cut out the shapes.

2. Glue 2 reindeer shapes together, aligning the edges. Let the glue dry.

3. Using a paintbrush, paint the entire reindeer with a coat of gesso. Let it dry thoroughly.

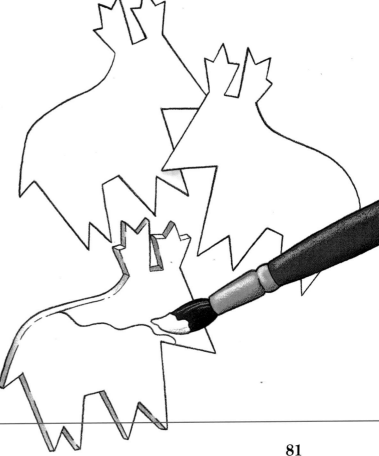

4. Paint the entire reindeer with 2 coats of paint in the desired color, letting the paint dry between coats. Paint the details as desired, letting the paint dry between colors. Let the reindeer dry overnight.

5. Using the black marker, make 2 eyes on the front of the reindeer.

6. Glue the pin back to the back of the reindeer. Let the glue dry.

Southwestern Sand Frames

Discover the ancient art of sand painting and create your own master pieces by spicing up plain photo frames with bold designs in colored sand. Choose from squiggly salamanders, electric arrows, fiery suns, nifty tepees, and cool green cacti.

You will need (for each frame):
Newspaper
Tracing paper
Pencil
Scissors
Precut, natural-colored, 2″-wide mat board
    frame
Small jar with lid for each color of paint
Powdered tempera paints in desired colors
White sand
Paintbrush
White glue
Photograph
Solid piece of mat board to match frame
    for backing

1. Before you begin, cover your work surface with newspaper.

2. Trace the desired patterns onto the tracing paper and cut them out. Trace the patterns onto the frame, arranging them as desired.

3. For each color used, fill a jar with 1 tablespoon of tempera paint and ½ cup of sand. Replace the jar lid tightly and shake the jar until the sand and the paint are blended together.

4. If desired, using the paintbrush, cover the area of the frame outside the traced shapes with a layer of glue. Sprinkle with white sand. Let the glue dry. Shake any excess sand onto the newspaper.
    Apply a layer of glue inside each shape. Sprinkle sand in the desired colors over the glue. Let the glue dry. Shake off any excess sand.

5. Arrange your favorite photo in the frame window and glue the remaining piece of mat board to the back of the frame.

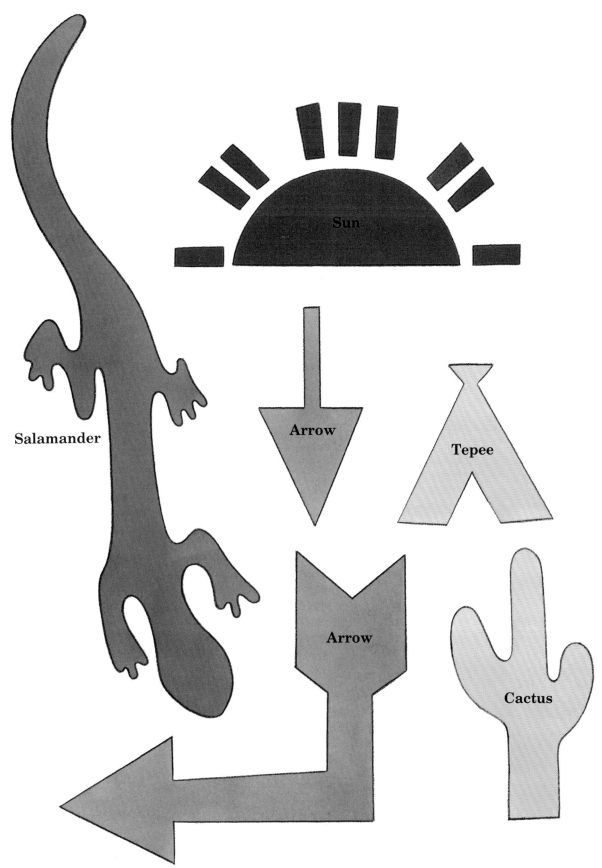

Salamander

Sun

Arrow

Tepee

Arrow

Cactus

Crunchy Pet Cookies

Treat your dog or cat to homemade cookies in tempting shapes and flavors. Bake a batch at Christmastime, or anytime, for a lip-smacking, pet-pleasing snack.

You will need (for 3 dozen bone or 2 dozen bell cookies):
A grown-up
Tracing paper
Pencil
Scissors
Mixing bowls: medium, small
2 cups of whole wheat flour
1 cup of yellow cornmeal
3 eggs
¼ cup of milk
Large wooden spoon
Rolling pin
Knife
Fork

Cookie sheets
Basting brush
For the bone cookies: ½ cup of beef jerky pieces
For the bell cookies: ½ cup of dried catnip

Craftivity to Go On

To make a special pet package for your cookies, use the bone or the bell pattern and follow the directions for Bag It and Tag It on pages 37–39.

1. Trace and cut out the desired pattern. Set it aside.

2. Combine the flour, the cornmeal, 2 eggs, and the milk in the medium-size bowl and stir until well blended. Add the beef jerky or the catnip to the mix and stir.

3. Roll out the dough onto a heavily floured surface. For each cookie, **ask the grown-up** to place the pattern on top of the dough and cut around it using the knife.

4. Using the fork, lightly beat the remaining egg in the small bowl until foamy.

5. Arrange the cookies on cookie sheets. Using the basting brush, lightly coat each cookie with beaten egg. **Ask the grown-up** to bake the cookies at 350° for 25 to 30 minutes or until lightly browned. Let the cookies cool.

Bell

Bone

Bubble Wand

Give your friends their very own bubble factory with giant wands that create hours of bubble-blowing good times. A wave of the wand sends short and squat bubbles or long and skinny ones drifting through the air—the size and the shape are controlled with a twist of the hand.

You will need (for 1 wand):
A grown-up
36″ (⅜″-diameter) wooden dowel
¼″-wide masking tape
Acrylic paints in assorted colors
Paintbrushes
Wooden bead with ⅜″ opening
Acrylic matte finish
60″ (⅜″) polypropylene cord
Liquid ravel preventer
1″-diameter plastic ring
Small rubber band
1 upholstery tack
Hammer
Plastic bucket
8 cups of distilled water
2 cups of liquid soap
1 cup of glycerin

Note: Bubble making is an outdoor activity. For best results, the temperature should be above freezing; in dry climates, the bubble solution may need more water.

1. Wrap the dowel with the masking tape to create stripes; then paint all the untaped areas with the desired colors. Set the dowel aside to dry. Paint the wooden bead with the desired color. Let it dry. Remove the tape from the dowel. Paint the bead and the dowel with the matte finish. Let them dry.

2. Treat both ends of the cord with liquid ravel preventer. Let the ends dry. To make the cord loop, insert 1 end of the cord through the plastic ring and pull 15″ of the cord through the ring. Holding both the short and the long lengths of the cord together, wrap the rubber band around the cord at the base of the ring to hold it in place.

3. Attach the cord to the dowel by sliding the ring over 1 end so that the short length of the cord is next to the dowel. Place the wooden bead on top of the dowel.

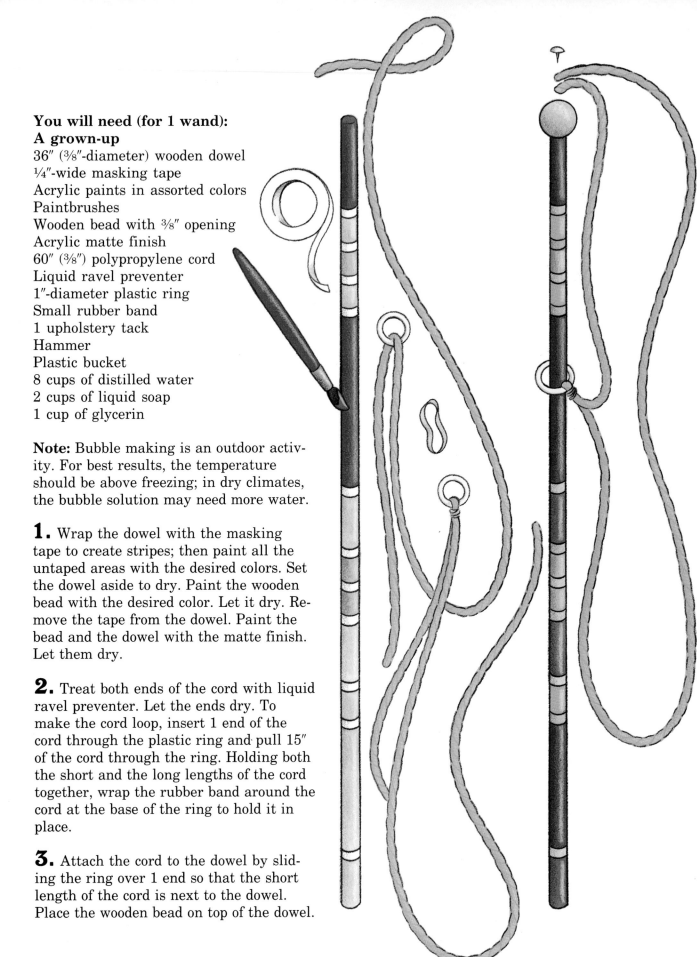

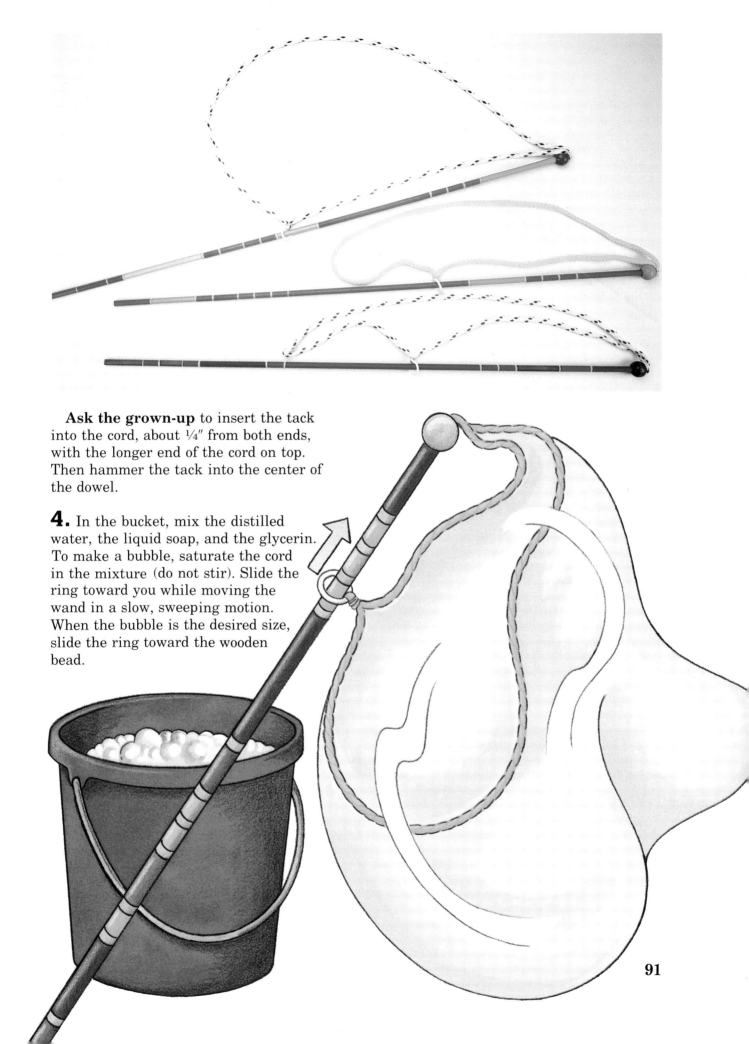

Ask the grown-up to insert the tack into the cord, about ¼″ from both ends, with the longer end of the cord on top. Then hammer the tack into the center of the dowel.

4. In the bucket, mix the distilled water, the liquid soap, and the glycerin. To make a bubble, saturate the cord in the mixture (do not stir). Slide the ring toward you while moving the wand in a slow, sweeping motion. When the bubble is the desired size, slide the ring toward the wooden bead.

91

Bauble Boards
& Knickknack Tacks

Gather loose game pieces, miniature toys, costume jewels, fishing lures, and any small souvenir you can find. Then attach them to a plain bulletin board and some thumbtacks to create your own kaleidoscopic collage.

You will need (for 1 board and tacks):
Assorted trinkets, buttons, and miniature toys
Founder's Adhesive glue
Bulletin board
Flat-head thumbtacks
For the ribbon board: polka-dot grosgrain ribbon

1. **For the ribbon board:** To determine how much ribbon you will need, measure completely around the edges of the bulletin board and add 8″ to the total. Glue the ribbon to the bulletin board, making a fold as you turn each corner. Let the glue dry.

2. Glue assorted trinkets, buttons, and toys to the edges of the bulletin board as desired. Let the glue dry.

3. Glue a trinket, a button, or a toy to the head of each thumbtack. Let the glue dry. Push the thumbtacks into the bulletin board.

Level 1

Ribbon Headband & Holder

Mirror, mirror, in my hand, who is the fairest in the land? You will be with this beribboned head-band! It only takes a few minutes to construct, so you can easily make some to keep and some to give away. And if you have a friend who has lots of headbands, make this handy holder for stackable storage on a dresser top.

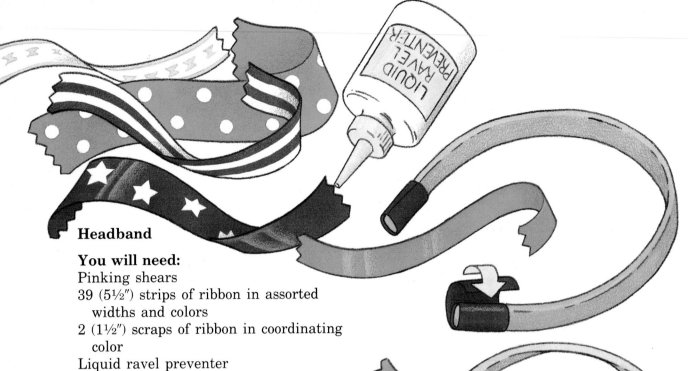

Headband

You will need:
Pinking shears
39 (5½″) strips of ribbon in assorted
   widths and colors
2 (1½″) scraps of ribbon in coordinating
   color
Liquid ravel preventer
¼″-wide plastic headband
Founder's Adhesive glue

1. Using the pinking shears, snip each
short end of the 5½″ ribbon strips. Apply
liquid ravel preventer to the cut ends.

2. Glue the 1½″ ribbon scraps around
the bottom ends of the headband to cover
the plastic tips.

3. To complete the headband, tie each
ribbon strip in a double knot around the
headband, alternating colors and widths,
until the headband is covered.

Headband Holder

You will need:
1 (18-ounce) empty rolled oats container
   with lid
½ yard of multicolored polka-dot fabric
Scissors
Fabric glue
Liquid ravel preventer
26″ (1″-wide) red-and-white polka-dot
   satin ribbon
¼ yard (⅛″-wide) red satin ribbon

1. Remove the lid from the container.
Cut a circle from the fabric to fit the inner

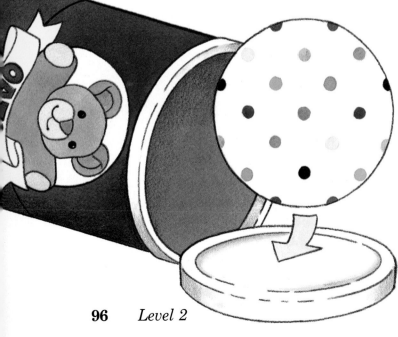

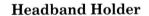

circle of the lid and glue it in place. Replace the lid on the container.

2. Cut a 7″ x 14″ strip from the remaining fabric. Apply liquid ravel preventer to the cut edges. Let them dry. Apply glue to the wrong side of the fabric along the edges. Wrap the fabric around the container, overlapping the raw edges in the back. Let the glue dry.

3. Cut the polka-dot ribbon in half. Wrap 1 strip around the top edge of the container, overlapping the ends and gluing them in place where the fabric overlaps at the back. Make sure that the top edge of the ribbon is even with the top edge of the container. Repeat with the remaining ribbon strip, gluing it to the bottom edge of the container and making sure that the bottom edge of the ribbon is even with the bottom edge of the container.

4. Tie the red ribbon into a bow. Glue it to the center front of the top ribbon strip.

Nuts About Magnets

Check out these funky magnet designs. All you need to make these animated characters come alive are a few items from the hardware store and some colorful beads. This dazzling duo's eyes catch the light and sparkle, while their bodies hold up drawings, photos, or invitations.

You will need
(for each magnet):

Tracing paper
Pencil
Scissors
White heavyweight paper
Paintbrushes
Founder's Adhesive glue
2 (¼″) hex nuts
Scraps of sisal rope
For the Santa: white, red, and black
    acrylic paints; 2 (8-mm) green faceted
    beads; 1 heavy-duty magnet
For the cat: aqua, pink, and white
    acrylic paints; 1 electrical switch box
    support for the body; 2 (8-mm) yellow
    faceted beads; 2 heavy-duty magnets

Santa Magnet

1. Trace and cut out the patterns. Trace the patterns onto the heavyweight paper and cut them out. Cut the legs along the broken line.

2. Paint the shapes as follows, letting the paint dry between colors: Paint the hands and the top and the bottom of the hat white. Paint the body, the center of the hat, and the mouth red. Paint the belt and the shoes black. Paint the belt tab white.

3. Glue the body to the back of the head. Glue the head to the back of the hat. Let the glue dry.

4. To make the eyes, glue 1 bead in the center of each hex nut. Let the glue dry. Glue the eyes in place.

5. To make the mustache, cut a 1″ piece of rope. Pinch the rope together in the center and glue it in place above the mouth. For the beard, cut a 2″ piece of rope. Separate the rope into individual strands and glue them under the mouth.

6. Glue the magnet to the center back of Santa's body. Let the glue dry.

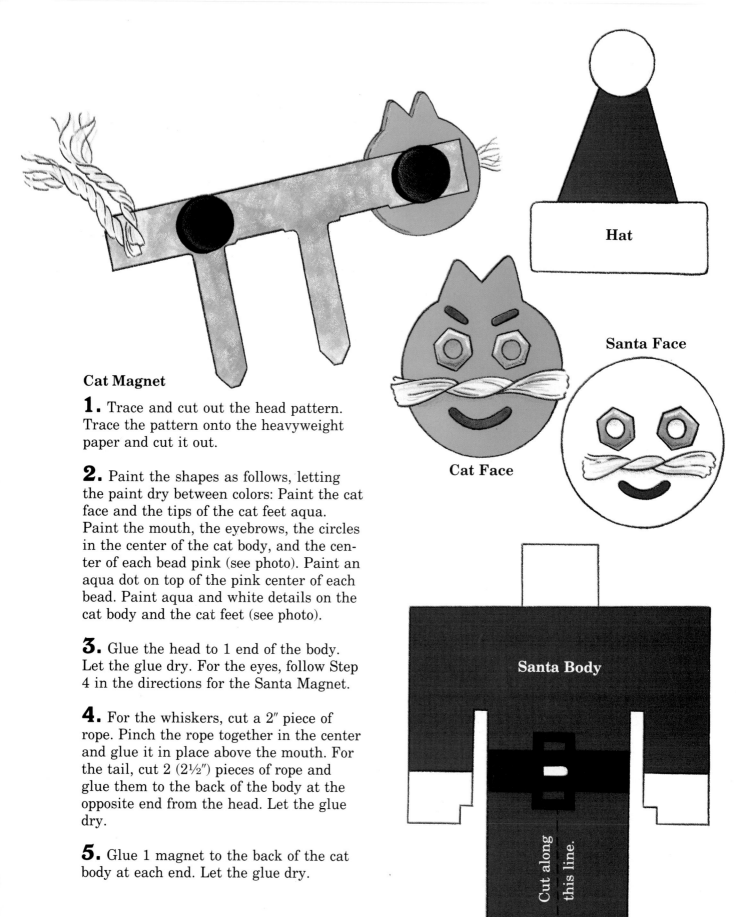

Hat

Santa Face

Cat Face

Santa Body

Cut along this line.

Cat Magnet

1. Trace and cut out the head pattern. Trace the pattern onto the heavyweight paper and cut it out.

2. Paint the shapes as follows, letting the paint dry between colors: Paint the cat face and the tips of the cat feet aqua. Paint the mouth, the eyebrows, the circles in the center of the cat body, and the center of each bead pink (see photo). Paint an aqua dot on top of the pink center of each bead. Paint aqua and white details on the cat body and the cat feet (see photo).

3. Glue the head to 1 end of the body. Let the glue dry. For the eyes, follow Step 4 in the directions for the Santa Magnet.

4. For the whiskers, cut a 2″ piece of rope. Pinch the rope together in the center and glue it in place above the mouth. For the tail, cut 2 (2½″) pieces of rope and glue them to the back of the body at the opposite end from the head. Let the glue dry.

5. Glue 1 magnet to the back of the cat body at each end. Let the glue dry.

Scented Soap Shapes

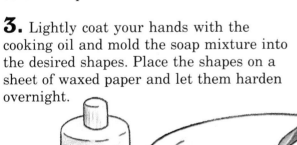

Pamper a friend with scented soaps molded into shapes such as balls, triangles, hearts, and squares. When bath time rolls around, these sweet-smelling delights will produce foamy, sudsy water.

You will need (for 6 small shapes):
Medium-size mixing bowl
1⅓ cups of gentle soap flakes
4 tablespoons of water
Large metal spoon
Food coloring in desired color
Scented oil
Cooking oil
Waxed paper

1. Mix the soap flakes and the water together, stirring to make a paste.

2. Add the food coloring and stir until the desired shade is achieved. Then add several drops of the scented oil. Mix well.

3. Lightly coat your hands with the cooking oil and mold the soap mixture into the desired shapes. Place the shapes on a sheet of waxed paper and let them harden overnight.

Take Note!

Make sure your message is received with an eye-catching note holder. Choose from the patterns you see here or dream up your own. There's no limit to the possibilities! Simply cut out two shapes from colored foam, decorate them any way you wish, and then glue them to a clothespin.

You will need (for each holder):
Tracing paper
Pencil
Scissors
Fun Foam in assorted colors
Wooden clothespin
Tacky glue
For the snowman, the house, and the tree: hole punch
For the package: ⅓ yard (¼″-wide) red polka-dot ribbon

1. Trace and cut out the desired pattern. Trace the pattern onto the foam 2 times. Cut out the shapes.

2. Trace the details, if any, from the pattern page onto the color of foam indicated and cut them out. (Some details don't need patterns; see below.) Referring to the photo, glue the details in place. **For the apple:** Glue the leaves to 1 side of 1 piece, 1 on top of the other, at the center top of the apple. **For the snowman:** Glue 1 hat each to the front and the back. Cut and glue 2 eyes. Use the hole punch to make 3 buttons; glue them to the front. **For the**

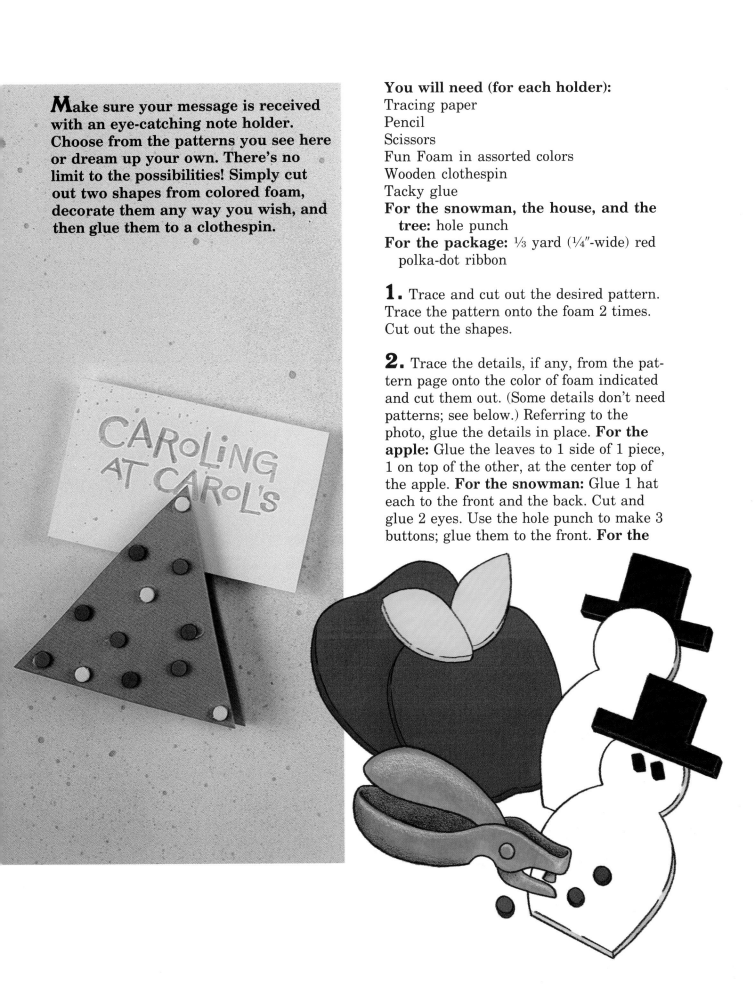

house: Glue the roof to 1 side of 1 piece. Cut and glue 2 windows and 1 door. Use the hole punch to make the door knob; glue it to the door. **For the tree:** Use the hole punch to make the ornaments; glue them to the tree as desired. **For the car:** Cut and glue 2 windows and 2 wheels. **For the package:** Cut the ribbon into 2 (3¼") strips and glue them to 1 side of 1 piece. Using the remaining ribbon, tie a bow and glue it onto the ribbon strip at the center top.

3. With the "mouth" of the clothespin facing up, glue the front and the back of the holder to the wide sides of the clothespin. Make sure that the bottom edges of the foam shapes are even with the straight edges of the clothespin.

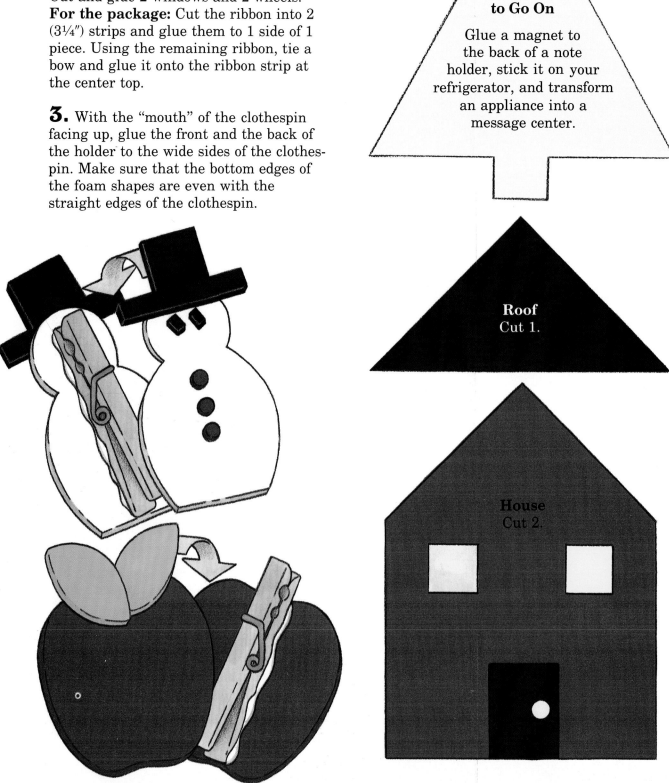

Craftivity to Go On

Glue a magnet to the back of a note holder, stick it on your refrigerator, and transform an appliance into a message center.

Roof
Cut 1.

House
Cut 2.

Hat
Cut 2.

Snowman
Cut 2.

Package
Cut 2.

Tree
Cut 2.

Leaf
Cut 2.

Apple
Cut 2.

Car
Cut 2.

105

Parents' Workshop
Great Gifts for Children

O Christmas Tree

There's nothing like the time-honored Christmas tree to bring the holiday spirit home. Celebrate this tradition with a quick-and-easy stylized tree that turns a plain outfit into a festive one.

You will need (for 1 tree):
Scissors
⅝ yard of green jumbo rickrack
Liquid ravel preventer
Purchased garment
Straight pins
Fabric glue
Thread: green, yellow
Sewing machine
White fabric paint
Needle
2″ yellow star button

1. For the tree, using the photo as a guide, cut the rickrack into 1 strip each of the following: 1 curve, 2 curves, 3 curves, 4 curves, 5 curves, and 6 curves. For the tree trunk, cut 2 strips of 3 curves each with a half curve at each end.

2. Apply liquid ravel preventer to the cut ends of all the rickrack strips.

3. To make the tree, center and pin the shortest rickrack strip approximately 2″ to 3″ below the neckband of the garment. Referring to the photo, continue pinning the graduated tree strips in place, approximately ½″ apart.

4. For the trunk, turn the cut ends under on the remaining rickrack strips and glue. Let the glue dry. Center the pieces under the tree and pin them in place.

5. Sew straight across the center of each rickrack strip.

6. Apply white fabric paint to the top of each rickrack tree strip, making sure the cut edges are covered by the paint (see photo). Do not paint the tree trunk pieces. Let the paint dry.

7. Using the yellow thread, sew the star button above the tree.

Starry-Night Dress

Create a dress especially for holiday outings using this unique yet simple counter-change technique. Counterchange is a type of pleaterless smocking that arranges stripes, dots, prints, or checks to form a design or pattern.

You will need:

Basic yoke dress pattern

Polished cotton fabric with ¼″-wide
   stripes (See pattern and note for
   yardage.)

Dressmaker's pen

18″ clear ruler with ¼″ markings

DMC embroidery floss: gold metallic;
   navy #823 and ecru for ladder stitch

#7 tapestry needle

#20 crewel needle

Note: Counterchange uses a 2-to-1 fullness ratio; if the yoke is 9″ wide, you will need 18″ of fabric for the finished width. (Cut out the remainder of the dress following the pattern instructions.)

Basic counterchange stitches include cable, trellis, and ladder stitches. Cable stitch is used for moving horizontally with borders. Trellis stitch is used for moving vertically and horizontally when forming a design. Ladder stitch is used to hold finished pleats in place and is worked from the front of the fabric.

1. Place the yoke on a flat surface. Beginning ⅝″ from the top raw edge, use the dressmaker's pen and the ruler to measure and mark the top and the bottom of the design (including the borders) with horizontal lines completely across the fabric. Between these lines, measure and mark horizontal lines ¼″ apart to form a grid on the fabric. Using the dressmaker's pen, mark the complete star design width of 83 stripes with vertical lines, counting from the center out and aligning each line with the edge of a stripe. (Changing the color of the starting stripe will alter the color of the star: begin stitching with a blue stripe for a white star or with a white stripe for a blue star. Make adjustments, if desired.)

For the sleeves: Using the dressmaker's pen and the ruler, measure and mark approximately 1¼″ from each short end,

aligning each line with the edge of a stripe. This is the area to be smocked. Beginning 1½″ from the raw bottom edge and working upward, measure and mark 4 horizontal lines ¼″ apart.

2. Following the instructions under the graph and using the gold metallic floss and the crewel needle, stitch the upper border, the stars, the background diamonds, the lower border, and the sleeve borders. Always work from the top to the bottom and from the left to the right unless otherwise noted. Refer to the diagrams for basic counterchange stitches.

3. When the design is complete, ladder-stitch each row, using matching thread and the tapestry needle.

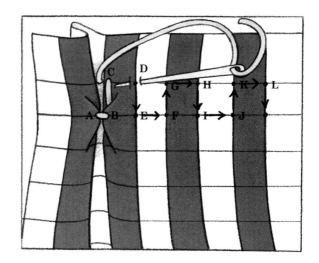

Cable Stitch

Working from the wrong side of the fabric, insert the needle at point A and pull the thread through to the front. Holding the floss below the needle, reinsert the needle horizontally at point A, taking a small stitch (2 to 4 threads) on each side of the stripe and moving from right to left. With the floss below the needle, move horizontally to point B and take another horizontal stitch; pull the thread loosely toward the left. Move vertically to point C and take another horizontal stitch, pulling the floss firmly to form a pleat. With the floss above the needle, move horizontally to point D and take a horizontal stitch. Move vertically to point E and take a horizontal stitch, pulling the floss firmly. Continue in this manner, leaving horizontal stitches loose and pulling vertical stitches tight.

cable stitch. If moving vertically more than ½″, take a vertical stitch to secure the thread and keep the stitches uniform (point X on the diagram).

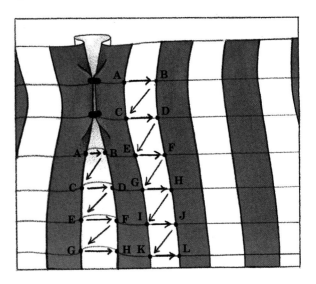

Ladder Stitch

Working from the right side of the fabric, take a small stitch at A and then at B; pull the stripes together. Take another stitch at C and then at D; pull the stripes together. Continue in this manner to complete each vertical row. This stitch may be worked from the top to the bottom or from the bottom to the top.

Trellis Stitch

Working from the wrong side of the fabric, stitches are taken horizontally as in the

112

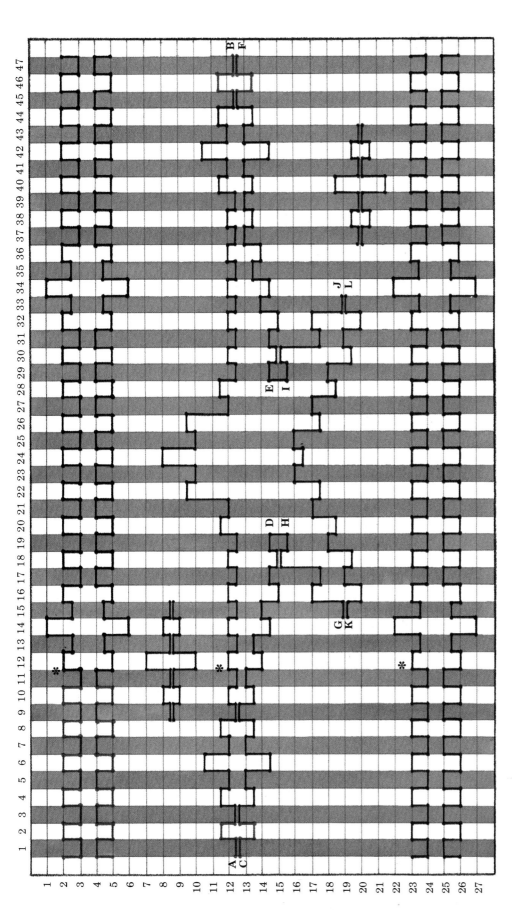

Upper border: Count back an even number of stripes from first marked vertical line. Following colored portion of border and beginning on row 2 with a down-stitch, stitch up to that line with single diamonds. Then continue as graphed to next vertical line (repeat begins at asterisk). Stitch single diamonds from second marked vertical line to seam allowance to fill. Begin row 5 with an up-stitch and repeat as above.

Stars: At the first marked vertical line, begin halfway between rows 12 and 13 with a down-stitch and follow graph from A to B. Continue to work in alphabetical order in a top-to-bottom pattern

to next vertical line (repeat begins at asterisk). Stitch colored portions only at beginning and end of design.

Triple diamonds: Begin with a down-stitch and continue as graphed. Place this design as desired.

Lower border: Repeat as for upper border, beginning on row 23 with a down-stitch. Begin row 26 with an up-stitch.

Sleeves: Repeat colored portion of upper border. Begin top row with a down-stitch. Begin bottom row with an up-stitch.

Holiday Vest

Your little helper will spread lots of Christmas cheer in this charming appliqué garment. All you need is a simple pattern, some festive fabric, and a handful of novelty buttons to make your holiday best vest just in time for Santa's visit.

You will need:
Purchased vest pattern
Cotton fabric: ivory, holiday stripe for lining
Straight pins
Scissors
Thread to match fabrics and felt
Sewing machine
Tracing paper
Pencil
Paperbacked fusible web: 10″ square, scrap
10″ square of green polyester felt
Iron
Pressing cloth
DMC pearl cotton floss #498 size 3
Large-eyed needle
Novelty buttons

Note: Cut the vest from a double thickness of the ivory fabric to keep the lining from showing through. To prevent dark print fabric from bleeding, soak it in equal parts of vinegar and water. Prewash all fabrics.

1. Following the manufacturer's instructions, make the vest.

2. Trace and cut out the patterns.

3. Following the manufacturer's instructions, fuse the 10″ square of web to the 10″ square of felt; fuse the scrap of web to the wrong side of a scrap of lining fabric. Trace the tree onto the fused felt and the tree trunk onto the fused fabric scrap. Cut them out.

4. Center the tree and the tree trunk on the vest back. Peel off the backing from the tree trunk piece and press it in place. Repeat for the tree, slightly overlapping the tree on the top of the tree trunk as shown. Cover both pieces with the cloth; press with a hot iron to fuse the patterns to the vest.

5. Referring to the diagram and using the pearl cotton, blanket-stitch along the edges of the tree and the tree trunk. Repeat to finish the edges of the vest.

6. Using the matching thread, sew the novelty buttons onto and underneath the tree as desired.

Blanket Stitch

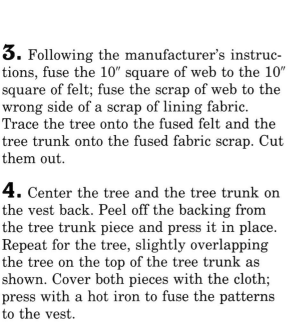

Tree

Tree Trunk

Rudolph Sweatshirt

This reindeer family is ready for Santa's sleigh ride! Yours will be, too, after a quick dash to the crafts store. Rudolph, with his snow-covered antlers and his nose so bright, is sure to spark some Christmas magic.

You will need:
Plain white paper
Black iron-on transfer pen
T-shirt board or piece of cardboard
Purchased white sweatshirt
Iron
Brown acrylic paint
Crystal fabric glitter paint
Paintbrushes
Black fabric paint pen
Large red acrylic jewel
2 (24-mm) wiggle eyes
Fabric glue
¾ yard (1½″-wide) plaid ribbon
Scissors
Liquid ravel preventer
Safety pin

1. Using the transfer pen, trace the reindeer pattern onto the paper.

2. Insert the cardboard form between the layers of the sweatshirt. Center the traced design facedown on the front of the sweatshirt. Following the manufacturer's instructions, iron the reindeer outline onto the sweatshirt.

3. Paint the face brown, leaving the mouth, the ear details, and the inside of the eyes and the nose unpainted. Paint the antlers with the glitter paint. Let the paint dry. Outline the entire reindeer with the black paint pen and paint the mouth and the ear details as indicated on the pattern.

4. Glue the nose and the wiggle eyes in place.

5. Tie the ribbon into a bow and trim the ends at an angle. Apply liquid ravel preventer to the cut ends. Attach the bow below the reindeer's chin with a safety pin. Remove the bow before laundering.

118

Candy Cane Cozies

Wrap up a sweet little girl in this scarf and earmuff duo. These warm fuzzies are a breeze to make and will provide cozy cover on those blustery winter days.

You will need:
Pencil
Tape measure
Scissors
Straight pins
Needle
White thread
Sewing machine
For the scarf: ½ yard of white acrylic or wool felt, 9″ x 50″ piece of red acrylic or wool felt, red embroidery floss, ⅝ yard (4½″-wide) white fringe
For the earmuffs: tracing paper, scraps of red felt, 4 (5″-diameter) circles of white felt, white embroidery floss, 2 (1″) white buttons, 2 (5″) strips of ¼″-wide elastic, purchased earmuffs

Note: Substitute polar fleece for felt and give your cozies a different texture.

Scarf

1. Cut the white felt into 3 (6½″ x 18″) strips.

2. Lay the red felt on a flat surface. Beginning 2½″ from 1 short end, pin the white strips diagonally on top of the red piece at 5½″ intervals.

3. Trim the edges of the white strips even with the scarf.

4. Using the red embroidery floss, blanket-stitch the white strips onto the red piece. For a blanket-stitch diagram, see Holiday Vest on pages 114–116.

5. Cut the fringe in half. Align 1 piece of fringe along each short end on the right side of the scarf. Turn the raw side edges under on each piece and pin the fringe

pieces in place. Using the white thread, machine-stitch the fringe to the scarf at each end.

Earmuffs

1. Trace and cut out the swirl pattern. Trace the pattern onto the red felt 6 times. Cut out the swirls.

2. For each side of the earmuffs, stack 2 white circles. Pin them together. Referring to the photo, pin 3 red swirls on top of the white circle in the shape of a peppermint candy. Using the white embroidery floss and a running stitch, sew the swirls to the white circle.

3. Stitch a button in the center of each circle where the points of the swirls meet.

4. Machine-stitch 1 (5″) strip of elastic to the outside edge of each circle, stretching the elastic to fit as you sew.

5. Cover the purchased earmuffs with the finished circles.

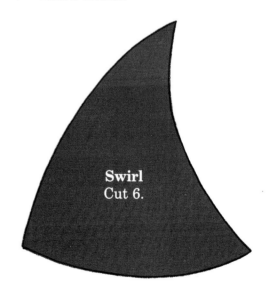

Swirl
Cut 6.

Hooded Pals Bathrobes

Create whimsical faces and floppy or pointy ears with easy appliqué on hooded robes. These bath-time buddies are sure to make getting out of the tub as much fun as getting in.

You will need (for each robe):
Tracing paper
Pencil
Scissors
Medium-weight and heavyweight fusible interfacing
Iron
Straight pins
Purchased hooded terry cloth bathrobe
Sewing machine
Dark pink thread
For the cat: scrap of dark green terry cloth, ⅛ yard of yellow terry cloth to match robe, ⅛ yard of pink terry cloth, yellow and brown thread, water-soluble fabric marker
For the dog: ⅛ yard of pink terry cloth; ¼ yard of medium blue terry cloth to match robe; scraps of dark blue, red, and tan terry cloth; red, dark blue, and white thread; white embroidery floss

1. Trace and cut out the patterns. Following the manufacturer's instructions, fuse the interfacing to the terry cloth, using the heavyweight interfacing for all ear pieces. Trace the patterns onto the colors indicated and cut them out.

2. Referring to the pattern for placement, pin the eyes and the nose in place on the front of the hood as follows. Machine-appliqué, using a zigzag stitch. **For the cat:** Pin 1 inner eye piece on top of each outer eye piece as indicated on the pattern. Use the yellow thread for the eyes and the dark pink thread for the nose. **For the dog:** Pin the tongue in place, overlap the top of the tongue with the muzzle, and then place the nose as indicated on the pattern. Use the red thread for the tongue, the dark blue thread for the muzzle, and the white thread for the eyes. Using 3 strands of the floss, satin-stitch the center and the corners of each eye.

3. For the ears, pin each inner ear piece to 1 outer ear piece. Machine-appliqué the inner ears in place, using a zigzag stitch and the dark pink thread; do not appliqué the bottom edges. **For the dog:** Referring to the pattern, pin matching ear pieces together.

To finish each ear, with raw edges aligned, stack 1 back ear piece on top of 1 front ear piece. Stitch them together, leaving an opening for turning. Turn and slip-stitch the opening closed. Press. Using thread to match the robe, topstitch outside the dark pink appliqué stitching.

4. To attach each ear, take a ¼" tuck in the hood from the inside (space the tucks evenly from the center top). Place the bottom edge of the ear inside the tuck and stitch the ear to the hood. This will create a seam without cutting the hood.

5. **For the cat:** Referring to the pattern, use the water-soluble marker to draw whiskers under the eyes and the nose. Using the brown thread, zigzag-stitch over the marked lines.

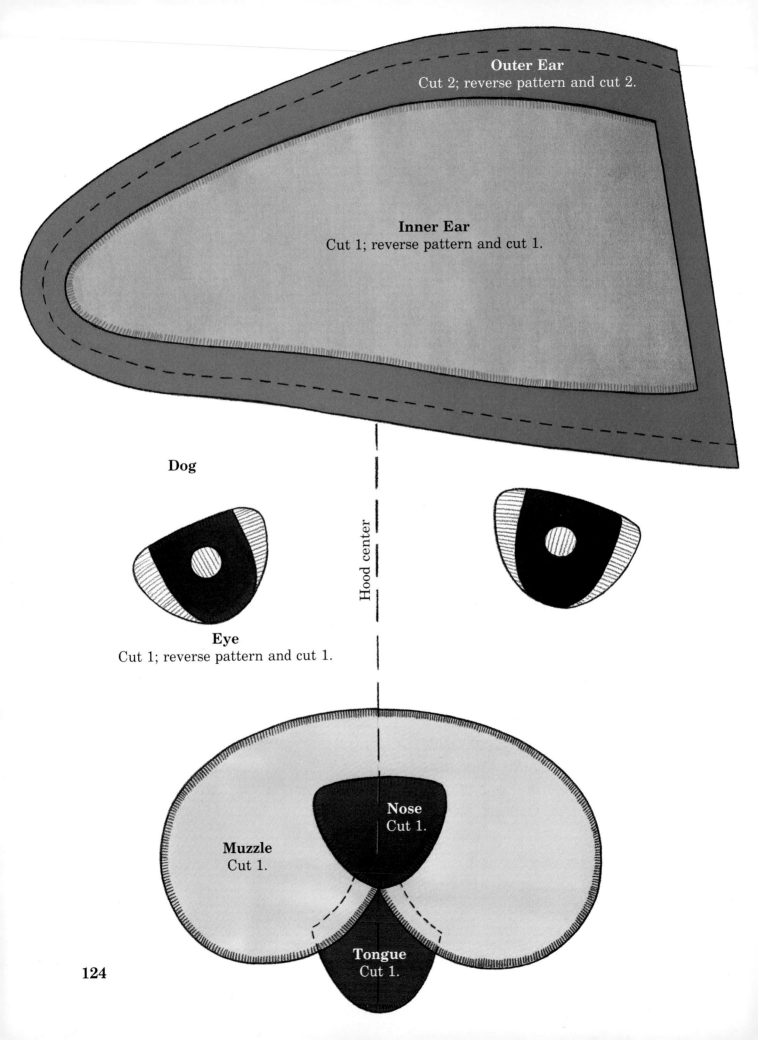

Outer Ear
Cut 2; reverse pattern and cut 2.

Inner Ear
Cut 1; reverse pattern and cut 1.

Dog

Hood center

Eye
Cut 1; reverse pattern and cut 1.

Nose
Cut 1.

Muzzle
Cut 1.

Tongue
Cut 1.

124

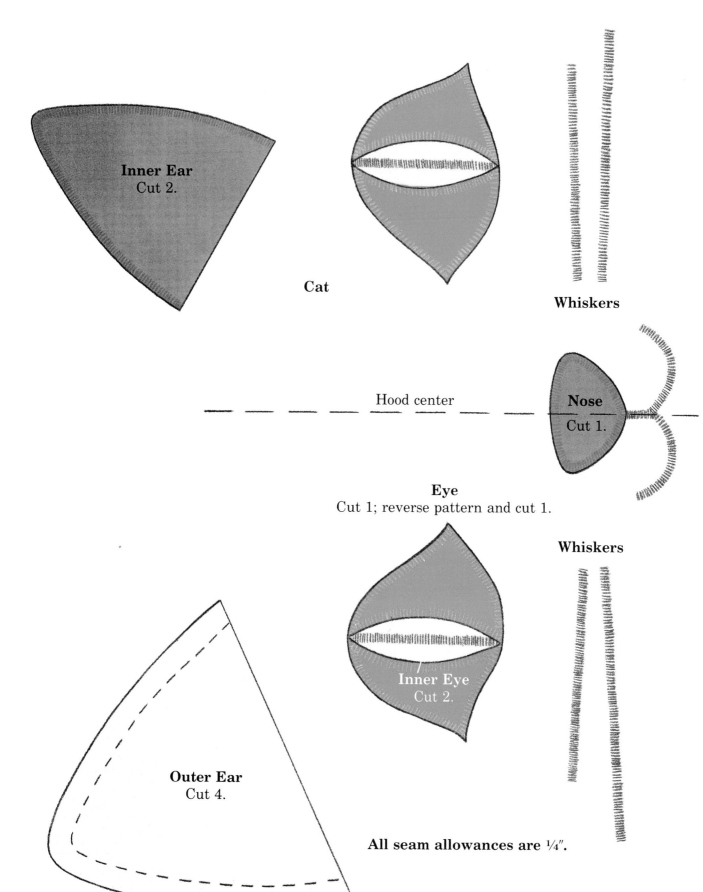

Inner Ear
Cut 2.

Cat

Whiskers

Hood center   **Nose**
Cut 1.

Eye
Cut 1; reverse pattern and cut 1.

Whiskers

Inner Eye
Cut 2.

Outer Ear
Cut 4.

All seam allowances are ¼″.

125

Tijuana Toy Box

Round 'em up! Decorate a storage box with a Southwestern twist and top it with blackboard paint for hours of imaginative fun. Then cowboys and cowgirls can corral those wandering toys in style.

You will need:
Tracing paper
Pencil
Scissors
Purchased wooden toy box
Fine sandpaper
White latex paint
Paintbrushes
Yardstick
Green blackboard paint
Acrylic paints: purple, red, yellow,
    orange, teal, brown, green, light
    green, black, pink, lavender
Clear acrylic varnish

1. Trace and cut out the borders and the patterns. Set them aside.

2. Lightly sand the toy box. Paint the box with the white paint. Let the paint dry and then apply a second coat. Let the toy box dry for several hours.

3. Leaving a 2″ margin on all sides, mark a large rectangle on the toy box lid. Paint the rectangle, using the blackboard paint. Let the paint dry.

4. Referring to the photo, trace the block border around the edges of the blackboard rectangle. Paint the border as indicated, alternating the colors for the center dot.

5. Trace the zigzag border around the base of the toy box, approximately 2″ from the bottom edge. Trace the patterns onto the toy box as desired and then paint them with the colors indicated.

6. Randomly paint small triangles and spirals on the toy box as desired. Let the paint dry overnight.

7. Apply a coat of varnish to the toy box. **Do not** cover the blackboard paint.

Coyote

Lizard

Zigzag Border

Cactus

Chili Pepper

Block Border

128

Flower Jump Rope

Want to send your little jumper bouncing over the flower tops? Get hopping with some colorful cording and a few pieces of fabric to put blooms in her hands and pep in her step!

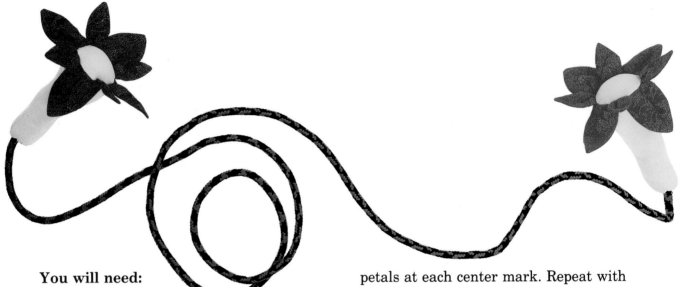

You will need:

Tracing paper
Pencil
Scissors
Straight pins
¼ yard each of cotton fabric: pink print,
  green, yellow
Thread to match fabrics
Sewing machine
Iron
Needle
2⅛ yard (⅜″-wide) pink-and-black nylon
  cording
Polyester fiberfill

1. Trace and cut out the patterns. Trace the patterns onto the fabrics as indicated, marking the center top on each stem piece. Cut them out.

2. For each petal, with right sides facing and raw edges aligned, sew 2 matching pieces together, leaving the bottom edge open. Then clip the curves and trim the tips. Turn the petals right side out and press.

3. On the right side of 1 stem piece, pin 1 large petal on each side of the center mark, pleating the straight edge of each petal slightly to form a tuck. Then pleat and pin 1 small petal between the large petals at each center mark. Repeat with the remaining stem and petal pieces. Machine-baste the petals in place.

4. With right sides facing, sew each pair of stem pieces together along the side seams, leaving the top and the bottom edges open. Pleat the straight edge of each of the remaining 4 small petals. Baste 1 in place at each side seam on the right side of the stems.

5. With right sides facing and raw edges aligned, sew 1 flower center to the top of each stem, catching all the petals in the seam.

6. Turn the flowers right side out. Run gathering threads around the base of each stem ¼″ and ⅛″ from the raw edge. Leave the ends of the thread long so that you can pull them later to gather the stem around the cording.

7. Adjust the cording length to suit your child. Knot each end; then tuck 1 knotted end into each stem. Stuff the stems firmly with fiberfill. Tuck under the raw edges. Then pull each set of gathering threads to secure each stem around the cording. Using the needle and the thread, secure the stems to the cording.

130

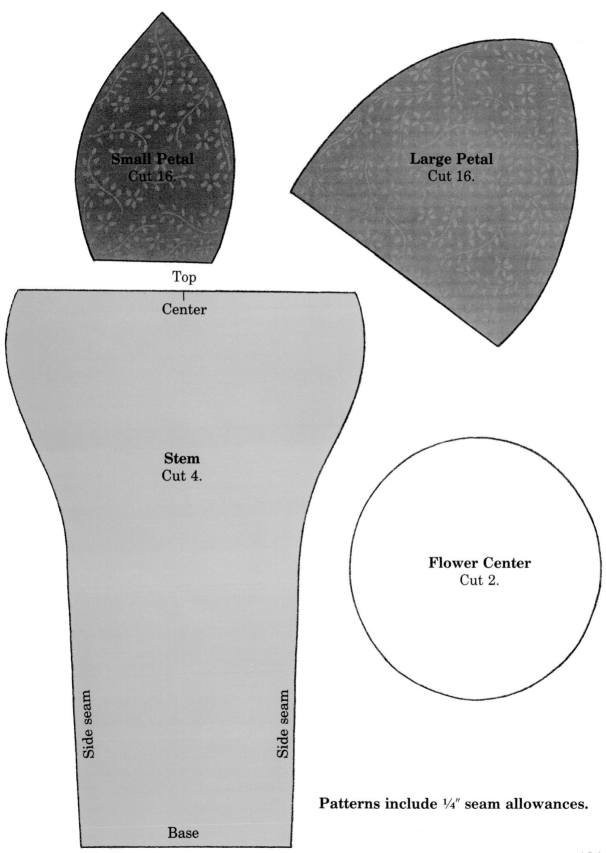

Small Petal
Cut 16.

Large Petal
Cut 16.

Top

Center

Stem
Cut 4.

Side seam

Side seam

Base

Flower Center
Cut 2.

Patterns include ¼″ seam allowances.

131

Frame a Face

Top a princess with a crown or a cowboy with a ten-gallon hat. Simply add a favorite photo to one of these whimsical frames and brighten up any spot in the house.

You will need (for each frame):
Tracing paper
Pencil
Scissors
Craft knife
Founder's Adhesive glue
Paintbrushes
9″ x 11″ piece of white mat board with a
    4½″ x 6¾″ opening
8″ x 10″ acrylic frame
For the crown: 10″ square of mat board;
    purple, gold, and pink acrylic paints;
    purple acrylic heart
For the cowboy hat: 7″ square of mat
    board; brown, red, white, and black
    acrylic paints

1. Trace and cut out the desired pattern. Trace the pattern onto the mat board square as indicated. Cut out the shape(s) using the craft knife.

2. Referring to the pattern, paint the shape(s) with the colors indicated. Let the paint dry between colors. **For the crown:** Glue the purple front on top of the gold back, aligning the bottom and the side edges. Set the shape aside.

3. Referring to the photo: Paint the 9″ x 11″ piece of mat board with the background color indicated. Let the paint dry. Trace the details onto the mat board.

Paint them as indicated. Let the paint dry.

4. Glue the 9″ x 11″ piece of mat board to the front of the acrylic frame, aligning the bottom edges.

5. Referring to the photo, center and glue the shape at the top of the mat board so that it slightly overlaps the inner edge. **For the crown:** Center and glue the heart at the bottom of the mat board. Let the glue dry.

6. Slide a photo into the frame.

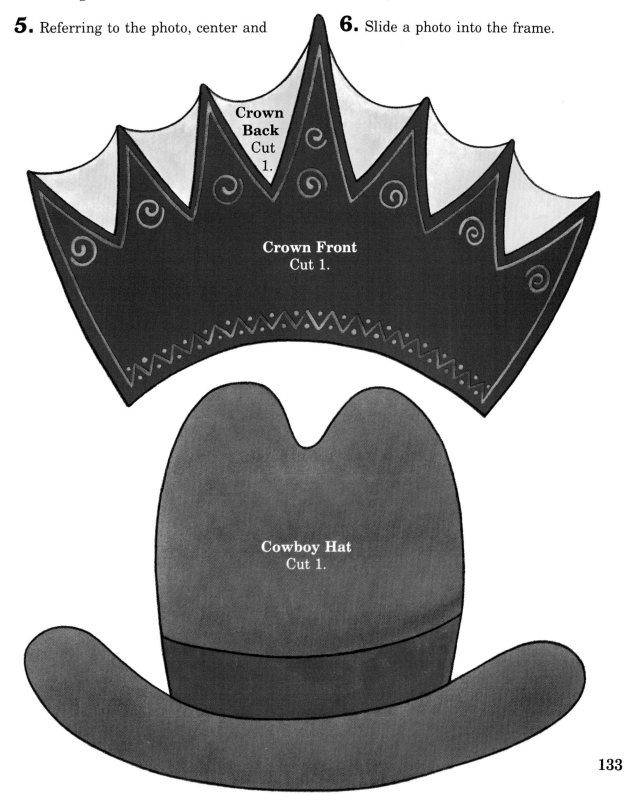

Crown Back
Cut 1.

Crown Front
Cut 1.

Cowboy Hat
Cut 1.

Checkerboard Play Mat

You've got this game in the bag! Spread out the play mat for a round of checkers and draw it up to create a tote. Kids can stuff it full of pj's and toys and carry it along on any outing.

You·will need:
1¼ yards of dressmaker's paper
Tape measure
Pencil
19″ piece of string
Pushpin
Scissors
45″-wide medium-weight cotton fabric: 2¼
   yards of blue, ¾ yard of white
Sewing machine
Blue thread
Straight pins
37″ square of low-loft batting
Large eyelet kit with 16 eyelets
Hammer
4 yards (⅜″-wide) red nylon cording
Liquid ravel preventer
Checkers game pieces: 12 red, 12 black
Small bag with closure

Note: All seam allowances are ¼″.

1. To make a pattern for the 36″-
diameter circle back, fold the dressmaker's
paper into quarters. Measure and mark
18″ along 1 folded edge, starting in the
corner where the folded edges meet. Tie 1
end of the string around the pencil and
the other around the pushpin, making
sure that the string in between measures

18″. Stick the pushpin into the corner where the folded edges meet. Pulling the string taut, place the pencil at the marked point and rotate the pencil along the paper until you reach the opposite edge, drawing an arc (Figure A). Cut along this line.

Figure A

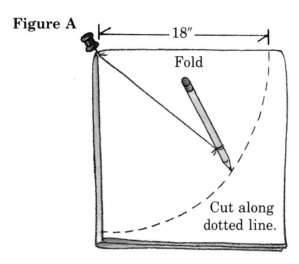

2. To make a pattern for the half-moon shapes, open the pattern for the 36″-diameter circle. Measure and mark 6¼″ from the top along the center fold. Draw a perpendicular line across the circle at this point (Figure B). Trace this half-moon shape onto a separate piece of dressmaker's paper and cut it out.

Figure B

3. From the blue cotton, cut 2 (2½″ x 42″) strips, 2 (1½″ x 16½″) strips, 2 (1½″ x 18½″) strips, 1 (36″-diameter) circle, and 4 half-moon shapes. From the white cotton, cut 2 (2½″ x 42″) strips, 2 (3½″ x 18½″) strips, and 2 (3½″ x 24½″) strips.

4. Sew the 2 (2½″ x 42″) blue strips and the 2 (2½″ x 42″) white strips together lengthwise, alternating colors. Cut this unit in half widthwise and sew the 2 sections together along 1 side edge, alternating colors (Figure C). Press the seams toward the blue strips.

Figure C

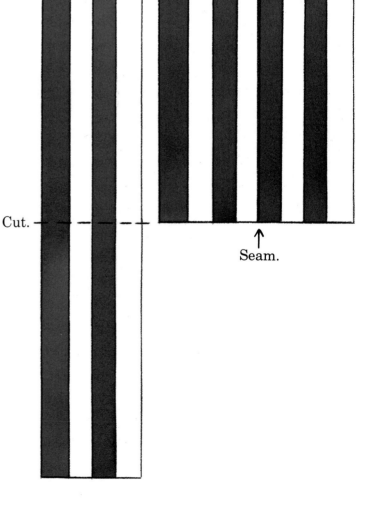

136

5. To form the checkerboard, use the marker and the ruler to draw straight lines across the colored strips at 2½″ intervals. Cut along the marked lines. Sew the cut strips together, reversing every other strip so that the squares are alternating colors (Figure D). Press all the seams in the same direction.

Figure D

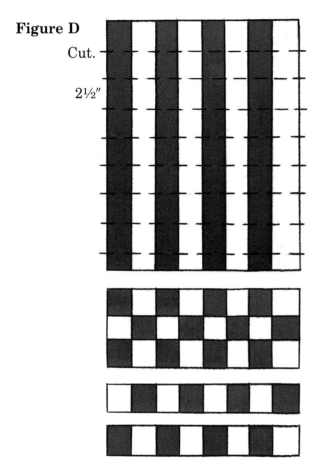

Cut.

2½″

6. Sew the 2 (1½″ x 16½″) blue strips to opposite sides of the checkerboard. Sew the 2 (1½″ x 18½″) blue strips to the remaining sides. Press the seams toward the blue strips.

7. Sew the 2 (3½″ x 18½″) white strips to opposite sides of the checkerboard. Sew the 2 (3½″ x 24½″) white strips to the remaining sides. Press the seams toward the blue strips.

8. Sew 1 blue half-moon shape to each side to complete the checkerboard top. Press the seams toward the blue shapes.

9. Stack the circle back right side down, the batting, and the checkerboard top right side up. Pin them together through all layers. Sew through all layers around the outer edge, leaving a 6″ opening for turning. Trim the edges close to the stitching line and clip curves. Turn and press.

10. Topstitch around the entire mat ⅜″ from the outer edge.

11. Stitch in-the-ditch between the half-moon shapes and the white strips and then between the white strips and the blue strips. Quilt the checkerboard on the diagonal both ways (see Figure E for a close-up of the checkerboard section). Then quilt around the perimeter of the checkerboard top.

Start quilting here.

Figure E

Start quilting here.

12. Measure 1″ from the outer edge and, following the manufacturer's instructions, apply eyelets at 6½″ intervals around the edge of the mat. Thread the cording through the eyelets. Tie each end of the cording in a knot. Apply liquid ravel preventer to the ends and let them dry.

13. Place game pieces in a small bag in the center of the mat. Pull the drawstring to close and tie the cording into a bow.

Making Waves

Accent a clear shower curtain with playful sea creatures in bold and vivid colors. Then make getting clean even more fun with a matching hand-painted shower brush.

You will need:
Tracing paper
Pencil
Scissors
Paintbrushes

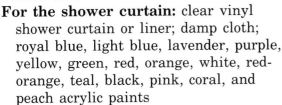

For the shower curtain: clear vinyl shower curtain or liner; damp cloth; royal blue, light blue, lavender, purple, yellow, green, red, orange, white, red-orange, teal, black, pink, coral, and peach acrylic paints

For the shower brush: wooden shower brush; red, yellow, green, and white acrylic paints; clear-drying varnish

Shower Curtain

1. Trace the patterns onto the tracing paper and cut them out.

2. Place the shower curtain on a clean, flat surface and wipe it with a damp cloth.

3. Referring to the photo, place the wave pattern underneath the shower curtain approximately 15″ from the bottom edge. Using the royal blue paint, paint the waves, staggering the pattern along the bottom edge and letting each wave dry before painting the next.

4. Randomly place the sea creature patterns underneath the shower curtain. Paint the patterns as indicated. Let the paint dry on 1 section of the shower curtain before moving to the next.

5. Hang the shower curtain in front of a white or bright-colored liner.

Shower Brush

1. Trace the small starfish pattern onto the tracing paper and cut it out. Trace the pattern onto the brush.

2. Paint the starfish as indicated. Decorate the brush with small dots along the handle and the sides. Let the paint dry.

3. Apply a coat of varnish to protect the finish.

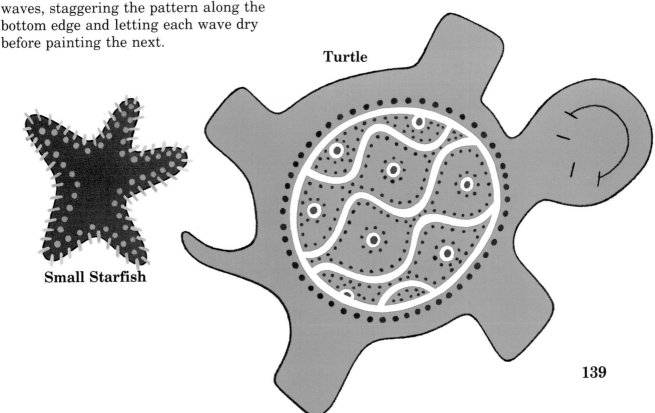

Turtle

Small Starfish

139

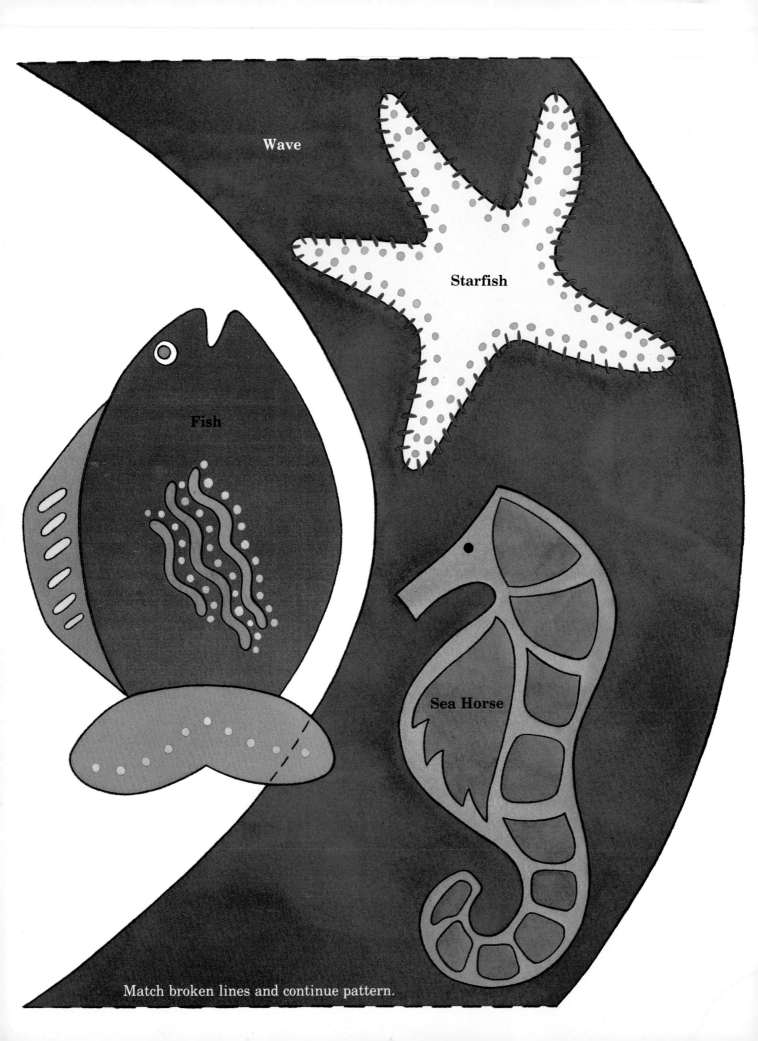

Wave

Starfish

Fish

Sea Horse

Match broken lines and continue pattern.